real greek food

real greek food

theodore kyriakou and
charles campion

photography by gus filgate

PAVILION

NOTE ON THE RECIPES

Most cookbooks are organised by ingredient, or by season, or by type of dish. *Real Greek Food* is somewhat different. This book is divided into the same number of sections as the menu at The Real Greek restaurant. Like the restaurant menu, it reflects some of the distinctive aspects of Greek dining. Greek meals are just not organised like everyone else's, as will quickly become apparent!!

ACKNOWLEDGEMENTS

To my parents, whose love of good food still inspires me. Our thanks to: Susan Campbell, Janie Suthering and Sandra Purkess for grappling with the recipes; Gus Filgate and Peter Thompson for stunning photographs, and Paul Welti for making the book look so good; Zoe Antoniou and all at Pavilion for their patience; Panos Manuelides for supplies; Paloma Campbell for her knowledge of Greek wines. And a special thank you to the backbone of the Real Greek kitchen brigade, Amanda Murphy, Alasdair Fraser, and Jodi Parsons. *Theodore & Charles*

The Real Greek Restaurant and Mezedopolio are at 14-15 Hoxton Market, London N1 6HG (020 7739 8212).

First published in Great Britain in 2000 by
PAVILION BOOKS

A member of **Chrysalis** Books plc

64 Brewery Road, London, N7 9NT

This paperback edition first published in Great Britain
in 2002 by Pavilion Books

Designed by Paul Welti
Page 190, courtesy of Peter Thompson, shows Theodore Kyriakou and
business partner Paloma Campbell

A CIP catalogue record for this book is available
from the British Library.

ISBN: 1 86205 625 0

Printed in Malaysia by Times Offset (M) Sdn Bhd

10 9 8 7 6 5 4 3 2

This book can be ordered direct from the publisher. Please contact
the Marketing Department. But try your bookshop first.

contents

preface

A very personal view by theodore kyriakou

When the Real Greek restaurant was still at the planning stage and I was jotting down my first

notes for the menu, I found myself wondering about the wisdom of going back to my roots and

putting them on a plate. Certainly I had never seen the kind of Greek food that I knew and

loved done justice in a restaurant setting and the trends all seemed to be about impressive and

variegated collections of unknown ingredients and flavours.

The Greek cooking that makes me feel homesick is a homely, honest and nostalgic kind of

food that is quite unlike anything you see in a career working in London restaurant kitchens. *Real*

Greek Food is about my return to "Arcadia", a place free of the commercially-exploited dishes. It

reflects the admiration I have for my parents and their devotion to Greek gastronomy.

In working on this book, (and on developing the restaurant) I find myself constantly

coming up against an insoluble contradiction – the image everyone else has of Greek food is so

very different to the way I remember the food that I grew up with. I want to set the record

straight. As my Father puts it, "When less than everything has been said about a subject, it is still

worth thinking a little further". *Real Greek Food* is my tribute to Greek cuisine. The recipes in it

come from all over Greece and from all kinds of people, but they are all about imaginative,

natural food and they all reflect the friendly hospitality that is our greatest national asset.

introduction

by Charles Campion

In the 5th century BC, while the British were donning woad and fighting among themselves,

Archestratus was busily engaged in writing Gastronomia, one of the world's first cookbooks. It

was read avidly in what was then the most civilized and sophisticated society in Europe – Greece.

So it comes as no surprise that when the rest of Europe began to value the new art

"gastronomy" (whose very name

Archestratus had foreshadowed), they took

Greek cuisine as their starting point. Indeed,

in 1825 Jean Anthelme Brillat Savarin's

masterwork, "Physiologie Du Goût" was

published, in which he observed that:

"Cooking and its amenities were held in high

esteem by the Athenians, as was natural in a race so elegant and eager for the new..."

In the twenty-three centuries between Archestratus and Brillat Savarin, tracking the cuisine

of Greece becomes a tale of invasions and assimilation, of different cultures and of merging and

refining. Greece has been invaded by Franks, Byzantines and Ottomans – it was part of the

Byzantine empire between 330 AD and about 1550, and then of the Ottoman empire until 1832

– and each of them has contributed to a very rich culinary heritage, and in more recent times this

mixture has been topped up by contributions from incoming Italians, Armenians and Turks.

The underlying resilience and strength of Greek cuisine stems from the fact that in Greece

there is no well-established restaurant culture. Everyone loves good food, everyone cooks at

home, and so there is no real need for restaurants. The social function is one that has been

taken over by the *kafeneion* or coffee house, until very recently a predominantly male arena

where gossip, alcohol, coffee, snacks and pastries are equally important. This happy

accident has meant that real Greek cuisine has been preserved by oral tradition, with simple

dishes being passed down from mother to child rather than the development of over-refined

recipes for use in fancy restaurants, targetting tourists instead of locals.

In a world that is fast beginning to realize the merits of healthier eating and simple, fresh,

tasty food ... *Real Greek Food* is a very exciting discovery.

"The dining table is the only place where we don't get bored during the first hour"
(Theo Kyriakou's mother offers her thoughts on Greek food throughout the book)

mezedes

THESE ARE SMALL DISHES, WHICH ARE A PRECURSOR TO THE MAIN MEAL.

YOU MAY HAVE A DOZEN SAUCERS, EACH WITH A SMALL PORTION OF A

PARTICULAR DELICACY. GETTING THE RIGHT COMBINATIONS OF THESE

DISHES IS AS CRUCIAL AS THE RECIPES THEMSELVES, BECAUSE A GOOD

SPREAD OF MEZEDES IS ALL ABOUT BALANCE. EACH RECIPE IS SUITABLE

FOR FOUR, WHEN COMBINED WITH THE RECOMMENDED ACCOMPANIMENTS,

UNLESS OTHERWISE STATED.

purée of yellow dal (fava)

φαβα

Fava is a great dish. When well-made, it is surprisingly light and fluffy due to the olive oil reacting much as it does in mayonnaise. The best kind of yellow split peas come from the volcanic island of Santorini, but if you cannot get hold of these then the next best thing is the yellow dal which is sold in Indian speciality shops. Only use the yellow split peas from supermarkets if you cannot get hold of either of the others. My mother says that "fava without spring onions is like a wedding night without games," so leave them out at your peril!

500g yellow dal

3 shallots, peeled and left whole

1 clove of garlic, peeled and left whole

2 bay leaves

150ml extra virgin olive oil

1 large bunch of spring onions

Enough fresh thyme to make 1 heaped tablespoon

Crusty bread to serve

Fresh lemon juice (if liked)

Sea salt and freshly ground black pepper

1 Rinse the dal thoroughly in a sieve under the cold running tap. (This will save you skimming later.)

2 Place the dal in a large, non-reactive saucepan with the shallots, garlic and bay leaves. Cover with plenty of water (about 3cm) and bring to the boil. Reduce to a simmer and stir occasionally to stop the mixture catching. Cook for about 35 minutes or until the dal has become very soft. Skim off any scum as necessary.

3 Drain the dal, but keep the cooking water. Remove the bay leaves, shallots and garlic and put the dal into a liquidizer with 100ml of the extra virgin olive oil. (Alternatively, you could use the fine disc of a hand-Mouli and finish off with a whisk.) Process until you have a very light, smooth and pale mixture (add a little of the cooking water if it seems too stodgy). Taste and season with sea salt and freshly ground black pepper.

4 Chop the spring onions finely, including the green parts, and strip the thyme leaves away from the stalks. Add them both to the mixture.

5 Serve the dal in a bowl and drizzle the remaining extra virgin olive oil onto the surface to prevent the finished dish from cracking like a dried-up river bed. Eat with plenty of crusty bread. (Some people like to add an extra squeeze of fresh lemon juice.)

What goes with what ...
To make up a well-balanced selection of mezedes, Fava should be teamed with some olives, some Dolmades, some good feta and some Lakerda (smoked fish). Traditionally, you eat Fava with large chunks of raw, sweet red onion. Here it is served with Horta.

onion-boiled eggs

This dish originates from the city of Thessaloniki and, according to my parents, it belongs to the recipes from the Greek Jewish community.

Onion skins from 15 Spanish
   onions (keep them in the fridge
   in a plastic bag until you've got
   enough)
6 medium eggs
6 tablespoons olive oil
1 tablespoon sea salt

1 Take half of the onion skins and use them to cover the bottom of a large saucepan.
2 Add the eggs and cover them with the remaining onion skins. Add the olive oil and salt.
3 Fill the saucepan with water, cover and bring to the boil. Turn the heat down to simmering point and leave to simmer for 4 hours, topping up with hot water if it looks like boiling dry. (This may sound strange but it's true!)
4 Let the eggs cool in the liquid.

What goes with what ...
For a good balance of mezedes, Onion-boiled Eggs should be served with the Potted Chicken with Walnuts, Aubergine Assanta and any leftovers from the Sunday roast.

aubergine assanta

This is another recipe which originates from the Greek Jewish community of the city of Thessaloniki. I remember trying this dish on the annual visit I made with my father to buy the year's supply of Kaseri cheese in a little town just the other side of the city.

250g dried chickpeas
500g Spanish onions, peeled and
    finely chopped
4 tablespoons extra virgin olive oil
600g aubergines
1 teaspoon powdered cumin
Sea salt and freshly ground black
    pepper

1 Soak the chickpeas overnight in a large bowl of water, add a pinch of salt. Discard the water and rinse under cold running water on the following day.
2 Take a pan and sauté the onions in the olive oil until soft, but not coloured. Add the chickpeas. Cover with water and bring to the boil. Turn down the heat to a simmer and cook uncovered until soft and done, about 30 minutes. Keep topping up with boiling water as necessary. This may take an hour or more. Strain off the water and set aside.
3 Preheat your oven to 200°C/400°F/Gas 6. Roast the aubergines, whole, on an oiled baking sheet until they are very soft. When they have cooled down enough to handle, remove the skins and mash the flesh in a bowl with a fork. Season the pulp with salt and pepper. Stir in the cumin and the chickpeas; mix together well.
4 Take a roasting tray (about 25 x 25cm x 5cm deep) and spread the mixture out evenly. Bake in the oven for about 30 minutes until done.

What goes with what ...
Aubergine Assanta goes well with spring onions or very finely sliced red onions, finely chopped mint or chervil. Do remember to be generous with the olive oil when you drizzle it over the top to prevent it drying out.

palace kiofte

These are the kings of the meatball world. The recipe originates from the Greek community in Asia Minor and was originally made for the Sultan!

80g lamb mince (ask your butcher
    to mince some shoulder finely)
80g belly pork (finely minced)
150g chicken leg meat (finely
    minced)
3 tablespoons very fine, white
    breadcrumbs
2 tablespoons finely chopped
    fresh mint leaves
1 bunch spring onions, finely
    chopped (including the green
    parts)
2 tablespoons roasted, salted
    pistachio kernels, coarsely
    ground
1 teaspoon freshly grated nutmeg
6 sheets filo pastry
50ml melted butter
Groundnut oil for frying
1 medium egg, beaten
Sea salt and freshly ground black
    pepper

1 In a large bowl knead together the three kinds of minced meat, bread-crumbs, mint, spring onions, pistachios, nutmeg and the seasoning. Cover and leave to rest for 1 hour in the fridge.

2 Take one sheet of filo, brush well with melted butter and superimpose the second sheet on top. Butter that one and add a third sheet. Arrange half the meat mixture along one of the edges of the filo sheet and roll it up like a fat cigar. Repeat with the other sheets of filo and the rest of the filling. Cover and put them in the freezer for about 1 hour so that they firm up.

3 Cut across each roll to give discs about 1.5cm thick. Heat the oil in a pan and, when it is hot but not smoking, dip the discs in the eggwash. Deep-fry them until they are golden brown, for about 3 minutes each side. Drain on kitchen paper.

What goes with what ...
These little meatballs make very good cocktail nibbles. If you are serving them as a meze, serve them with Cheese Triangles, Dolmades and Tzatziki.

purée of aubergines

This is one of the few occasions when food processors are banned! In this meze, the right texture can only be created by preparing the dish by hand with a knife.

500g aubergines

50g shallots, peeled and finely chopped

1 clove of garlic, peeled and crushed

100g fresh plum tomatoes, peeled, deseeded, and diced

1 heaped teaspoon fresh flat-leaf parsley, very finely chopped

1 heaped teaspoon fresh coriander, very finely chopped

50ml extra virgin olive oil

A squeeze of lemon juice

Sea salt and freshly ground black pepper

1 Over a gas burner, on a barbecue or under the grill, char the aubergines thoroughly. When well coloured, peel and chop the flesh very finely with a knife. Transfer to a bowl and as you do so, add the shallots, garlic, tomatoes (they must be fresh, tinned ones will not do), and the herbs.

2 Mix together with the oil and lemon juice before seasoning with salt and pepper to taste.

What goes with what ...
This dip goes well with Pastourma (cured meat), Purée of Smoked Red Peppers with Feta and Octopus in Red Wine.

purée of smoked
red peppers with feta

This is a Thracian meze. Be careful not to overdo the mixing or it will turn to mush. It is also important to start off with a good-quality Greek feta cheese, preferably one that has been matured in oak barrels. If you cannot obtain the Greek aged red wine vinegar, substitute balsamic or juice from pickled peppers.

125g red onions

6 tablespoons extra virgin olive oil

350g fresh or smoked red peppers
  available in jars

300g good Greek feta cheese

2 tablespoons aged Greek vinegar
  (or if you are using peppers
  from a jar, substitute
  2 tablespoons of the juice)

1 teaspoon fresh thyme leaves

Sea salt and freshly ground black
  pepper

1 Preheat your oven to 200°C/400°F/Gas 6.

2 Put the onions on a baking sheet, and roast in their skins for about 45 minutes or until soft.

3 If you are preparing your own peppers, char them either over a gas burner, on a barbecue or under the grill. When black, put them straight into a plastic bag and let them cool down. Take them out and you will find that the skins will rub off easily.

4 Deseed and finely chop the peppers and finely chop the onions. Place in a bowl and mash together with the cheese. Add the oil, vinegar and thyme; season and mix together. The perfect texture is similar to that of a coarse meat paste.

What goes with what ...
This dip goes well with
Pastourma (cured meat),
Purée of Aubergines and
Palace Kiofte.

τυροπιτάκια
cheese triangles

This is a recipe from Alexandroupoli, which is the last major Greek city on the way to Turkey. It is a part of the world that is famous for its buttery pastries and these are very good indeed.

100g Greek feta

100g Kaseri (or very mature Cheddar cheese)

100g Graviera (or mature Gruyère cheese)

4 medium eggs

3 heaped tablespoons finely chopped fresh mint leaves

$^1/_2$ a nutmeg, grated

Freshly ground black pepper

500g filo pastry

100g butter, melted

500ml whole milk

100g cold butter

1 Preheat your oven to 180°C/350°F/Gas 4.

2 Grate all the cheeses into a mixing bowl. Add two of the eggs and, with a hand blender, turn the mixture into a purée. Add the chopped mint, nutmeg and black pepper; mix well. The mixture should not require additional salt as the cheeses are salty enough already.

3 Take two sheets of filo, brush one generously with melted butter and lay the other exactly on top. Cut this "sandwich" into strips of approximately 5 x 20cm. Put a tablespoon of the cheese filling in the centre of the strip, about 2cm from the end. Fold one corner over in a triangle. Fold in the edges about $^1/_2$cm, then continue turning over the triangle until you reach the end of the filo strip, buttering it well with each turn.

4 Continue making pastries until you have finished up all the cheese mixture and arrange them on an oiled baking sheet with a rim.

5 Beat the milk with the two remaining eggs in a bowl and pour the liquid over the pastry triangles. Leave the pastries to stand, uncovered at room temperature, until all the liquid has been absorbed. Place one small knob of cold butter on each triangle and bake in the oven until they are golden, about 35–40 minutes.

What goes with what ...
Because these pastries are so rich, they go very well with Purée of Aubergines and Purée of Smoked Red Peppers with Feta, as shown.

roast pork nibbles

On the Thursday before Lent most Greek eating houses stoke up a mighty barbecue and these delicious bits of meat from the pig's head are one of the star attractions. This particular Thursday is even known as "smokey barbecue day". The Friday immediately afterwards you can see clothes hanging out on terraces all over town in a vain attempt to get rid of the smokey smells of barbecued meat!

Half a pig's head (ask your
    butcher)
4 litres water plus 600g salt and
    400g sugar
2 cloves of garlic, peeled but left
    whole
3 bay leaves
500g white bread, cut into thick
    slices
50ml olive oil
Juice of 1 lemon
Sea salt and freshly ground black
    pepper

1 Soak the pig's head in the brine for 24 hours (or for up to 3 days if you have got the time).

2 Preheat your oven to 200°C/400°F/Gas 6.

3 Remove the pig's head from the brine and dot with the garlic and bay leaves. Surround the head with the thickly sliced bread, which will absorb all the fat during cooking, and wrap it in plenty of baking parchment. Tie the parcel up with butcher's string and bake it in the oven for 3–3$^{1}/_{2}$ hours.

4 Open the parcel, throw away all the bread and use a fork to scratch off all the meaty bits of pork into a bowl. Pick the remaining meat from the head. Add the olive oil and lemon juice, then season the mixture and mix together.

What goes with what ...
This dish is a meze to serve on its own with drinks – you don't eat it with other dishes. It makes the perfect partner to Ouzo or a full-bodied red wine. Any leftovers will cook up well with egg tagliatelle or rice.

"The smell of a good dish is both tangible and edible"

χοιρινα παϊδακια απο την κοιλια με πρασα

belly pork with leeks

This is a typical winter meze, which comes from the rural part of the Peloponnese. After the men have spent the whole day in the fields collecting the maincrop potatoes for the winter, this dish is a welcome filler.

2 tablespoons olive oil

50g butter

1kg belly pork (ask your butcher to bone it out and cut it into 1cm cubes)

150ml red wine

700g leeks (slice them finely and use the white parts only)

Sea salt and freshly ground black pepper

1 Place the olive oil and butter in a frying pan over medium heat and when frothing, add the pieces of meat and cook them for a few minutes, stirring so that they do not catch, until golden brown. Flame the pan with the red wine.

2 Add the leeks and adjust the seasoning. Cover the pan, turn the heat down and cook until the leeks start falling apart and taste very sweet. The secret is to cook the mixture until the leeks have melted down to a sauce, which will take about 45 minutes.

3 Check the seasoning again (be generous with the black pepper) and serve the dish immediately.

What goes with what ...
This hearty dish goes well with plenty of warm sour dough bread and a bottle of cold beer or red wine. It is sometimes known as "wine meze".

octopus in red wine

It's an enduring image of Greece, and one much beloved of travel agents the world over: the sun sinks into the Western Sea and in the foreground an old Greek fisherman is beating an octopus to tenderize it on a rock. This dish works just as well with an octopus from your fishmonger, especially as the frozen octopus usually come already tenderized!

500g Mediterranean octopus
220ml red wine
100ml red wine vinegar
¼ teaspoon cumin powder
4 tablespoons extra virgin olive oil
Freshly ground black pepper

1 Cut the octopus into small, 2cm chunks. In a large bowl, mix together the red wine, red wine vinegar and cumin. Add the octopus pieces and leave them overnight in the refrigerator to marinate.

2 Remove the octopus from the marinade and place it in a large saucepan. Cover and cook it over a low heat without water or oil. Check after 10 minutes: the octopus should have started to lose water. Stir and cook on for another 45 minutes or until the octopus is tender.

3 Drain the octopus from the cooking liquid and add the liquid to the marinade. Take a frying pan and add the olive oil. Sear the octopus for 5–8 minutes, then flame the pan with the marinade. Cook the octopus fiercely for a few more minutes, until most of the liquid is evaporated and you've got just a bit left over to use as a sauce.

4 Season with black pepper, but do not add salt as the octopus is naturally salty, and serve with the sauce.

What goes with what ...
This meze goes well with Horta, Fava and plenty of bread for dipping in the juices.

crisp-fried okra

As an alternative to the vinegar soak used in this recipe (which is said to help get rid of the glueyness of the okra), my mother used to leave the okra out on the back porch in the heat of the sun, which seemed to do the trick. There is no sun in some countries, but there is vinegar so the recipe is still a good one.

1kg okra
300ml white wine vinegar
1 litre groundnut oil for frying
Cayenne pepper, to season
Sea salt and freshly ground black pepper

1 With a paring knife, trim the stem ends of the okra without opening the pods. Take a large bowl, add the vinegar and drop in the trimmed okra. Toss the okra in the vinegar and allow to stand for at least $1/2$ hour and up to a maximum of 1 hour. Dry the okra pods on kitchen paper, then cut them into 1cm pieces.

2 Heat the groundnut oil in a deep fat fryer or saucepan until its surface starts to tremble. Fry the okra by scattering it into the oil a little at a time (if you add too much at a time the temperature will drop too abruptly and you will never get crisp okra). Leave the okra in the oil for 2–3 minutes or until it is a burnished brown. Remove with a slotted spoon and drain on kitchen paper. Sprinkle with salt and the two peppers.

What goes with what ...
Serve the okra while still hot with really garlicky Skordalia and plenty of cold beer. Even when we were very young, this was our favourite snack after swimming – perhaps because my mother would give us red or rosé wine diluted with soda water. This is the ultimate nibble with drinks.

parchment-wrapped liver

This recipe comes from Epirus. For a true flavour of Greece all you need is some of this dish, plenty of sour dough bread and a heated argument!

3 tablespoons fresh thyme leaves

1¹/₂ bunches spring onions, finely chopped (including the green parts)

60g Kalamata olives, pitted and finely chopped

200g plum tomatoes, peeled, deseeded and finely chopped

100g green peppers, deseeded and finely shredded

1 lemon, cut into 8 wedges

2 tablespoons fresh, flat-leaf parsley, finely chopped

100ml extra virgin olive oil

1kg liver (calf's liver is the most expensive option, lamb or pork liver being the cheaper alternatives), membrane removed and sliced into 6 portions (ask your butcher)

Sea salt and freshly ground black pepper

1 Take a large mixing bowl and add the thyme leaves, spring onions, olives, plum tomatoes, green peppers, the unsqueezed lemon wedges, parsley and olive oil. Mix well and add the liver. Season with salt and pepper. Cover with cling-film and refrigerate for at least 1 hour (and up to 2 hours, if possible) to allow the different flavours to penetrate the liver and so that the vegetables start to lose some of their water.

2 Preheat your oven to 180°C/350°F/Gas 4.

3 Cut out three pieces of baking parchment (about 60cm) square and layer them one on the top of the other. Arrange the liver slices in the middle of the paper with all the other ingredients, then fold it up like a parcel. Secure with butcher's string, place in a roasting tray and bake for about 40 minutes, depending on just how pink you like your liver.

What goes with what ...
This is another of the more heavy "wine meze" and you can get away with serving it with nothing more complex than some homemade chips.

stuffed vine leaves

ντολμαδακια γιαλαντζι

Dolmades are a typical part of the first meal of Lent, eaten on the day known as "Clean Monday". They originate from Macedonia and are quite fiddly to make, but well worth the effort. Make the dolmades small, about two bites worth and no more than 4cm long. This recipe makes 15–20 dolmades. The rice soaks up the liquid as it cooks so measure out all your quantities carefully and you should get the result you are after.

200ml extra virgin olive oil

70g shallots, peeled and chopped

1 bunch spring onions, finely chopped (include most of the green parts)

1 clove of garlic, peeled and crushed

120g short-grain rice

1 heaped tablespoon finely chopped dill

1 level tablespoon finely chopped flat-leaf parsley

40g sultanas

40g pine kernels

Juice of 1 lemon

200ml hot water

1/2 a jar of preserved vine leaves (you'll need 15–20 leaves)

Sea salt and freshly ground black pepper

1 Heat 100ml of the oil in a large non-reactive pan. Add the shallots and spring onions; cook until soft, but do not allow to colour. Add the garlic after about 5 minutes. Keep the ingredients in the pan moving and sauté as you add the rice, dill, parsley, sultanas, pine kernels, lemon juice and the remaining oil. Season with salt and pepper. Finally, add the hot water.

2 Cover the pan and leave to simmer for 5 minutes. Remove from the heat and allow to cool.

3 Soften the vine leaves in boiling water (this will take about 15 minutes), drain and refresh in cold water. Allow to cool and you are ready to roll!

4 Place each leaf, shiny side down on a board and add 2 teaspoons of the mixture. Roll up, then turn the sides in to make a neat and well sealed parcel. As you complete each parcel, place it, join side down, in a pan with a lid. (Place a plate on top of the parcels to keep them firmly pressed down so that they do not unravel when cooking.) Cover with water, add the remaining 100ml of oil and bring to the boil. Turn the heat down to a simmer and put the lid on. Cook for 30–45 minutes, or until the rice is tender and has absorbed most of the water.

5 Leave the dolmades to cool down, cover and then refrigerate. They will keep for 5 days. Allow them to come back up to room temperature before serving so that the flavours can develop properly.

What goes with what ...
The natural partner to Dolmades is Tzatziki. In addition, try Pan Fried Kefalotiri, Potted Chicken with Walnuts or smoked fish.

pan fried kefalotiri

Kefalotiri is a splendid Greek cheese that is made from ewe's milk and it is similar in character to the Italian Pecorino. It is made both on Crete and in Epirus, and is seasonal. If you are unable to obtain Kefalotiri, it is better to substitute Pecorino than Halloumi cheese, which can end up being rubbery in texture and tasting very salty.

50g unsalted butter
60ml olive oil
300g Kefalotiri cheese
A large bowlful of iced water
Flour seasoned with sea salt and
  freshly ground black pepper,
  for coating the cheese

1 Heat the butter and oil together in a frying pan.
2 Meanwhile, cut the Kefalotiri up into narrow fingers and put them in a bowl of iced water for 30 seconds. This will make the flour stick to the cheese and help to form the crust.
3 Roll the cheese in the seasoned flour and fry until crisp and golden on the outside, with the cheese melting inside. Serve promptly while still very hot.

What goes with what ...
This dish must be eaten hot so whatever you decide to team it with, you should always eat the Kefalotiri first! It will go well with a squeeze of lemon, Potted Chicken with Walnuts, Horta and Tzatziki.

potted chicken with walnuts

This dish originated in the area of Asia Minor that is now known as Western Turkey and teams chicken with walnuts. It is presented in multiple layers, each one of a different texture. Sometimes known by the less elaborate name of "Eastern Chicken", it is a rich concoction and the eastern flavour of cumin betrays its origin.

1 chicken (about 1.5kg)
200g white bread (cut off the
  crusts)
300g walnut kernels, finely
  ground and toasted in a dry
  pan with cumin (see below)
100ml chicken stock
2 cloves of garlic, peeled and
  crushed
1 tablespoon toasted cumin seeds
  (see introduction)
2 tablespoons finely chopped
  fresh coriander
75ml extra virgin olive oil
1/4 teaspoon cayenne pepper
Sea salt and freshly ground black
  pepper

1 Put the chicken in a large, deep saucepan and cover with water. Bring to the boil and then simmer with the lid on until cooked, about 25–30 minutes. (Do not continue to boil or the chicken will become tough.)
2 Remove the chicken from the pan and when cool enough to work with, skin it and remove all the bones. Shred the meat with a fork.
3 Soak the bread in water, then squeeze it and put it in a blender or food processor together with the walnuts, chicken stock, garlic, cumin and coriander. Process until mixed, season and divide into two portions of roughly one third and two thirds.
4 In a bowl, mix the chicken with two thirds of the walnut mix and either pack it into the bowl in which you are going to serve it or into a number of small individual ramekins.
5 Add the remaining walnut mix as a second layer and press down firmly with your fingertips.
6 Mix the oil and cayenne pepper together thoroughly and use this as a final layer. Cover and refrigerate. Serve at room temperature.

What goes with what ...
Serve with the Pan Fried Kefalotiri cheese and Dolmades, as shown here.

tzatziki

This is a simple dish, but it is all too easy to get it wrong. In Greece my mother would sometimes serve it with a few ice cubes in the bottom of the bowl (as is sometimes done with Gazpacho), and that provided the cooling element to a meze. The acidic qualities of the crushed garlic develop with time and tzatziki will become stronger the longer you leave it. Up to three days old, it is still delicious but after that time it can become very strong. Use thick Greek yoghurt if you can.

1 cucumber
250g thick Greek yoghurt
2 tablespoons extra virgin olive oil
4 cloves of garlic, peeled and
   crushed
1 tablespoon finely chopped fresh
   mint
Sea salt and freshly ground black
   pepper

1 Peel, deseed and finely dice the cucumber. Be careful to get rid of all the seeds or they will give the finished tzatziki a watery texture.
2 Mix together the yoghurt, oil, garlic and mint in a bowl. Season to taste with salt and pepper. Refrigerate for at least a day to let the flavours develop.

What goes with what ...
With the Tzatziki, serve Pan Fried Kefalotiri cheese. Other good matches are spicy Pastourma (cured meat), Purée of Smoked Red Peppers with Feta and the special Bread Stuffed with Spinach and Cheese.

skordalia

A simple but satisfyingly pungent Greek "super-aioli", which goes well served as a relish with rich food. For a special treat, why not try adding 100g ground almonds to the final mix? This is how they do it near the lake of Ioaninna, where freshwater crayfish with almond skordalia is a local speciality.

750g floury potatoes
4 cloves of garlic
1 tablespoon fresh lemon juice
175ml extra virgin olive oil
1 medium egg
Sea salt and freshly ground black
   pepper

1 Boil the potatoes in their skins until cooked – about 30 minutes. You want to end up with starchy mashed potato. Peel them when they are cool enough to handle and mash or put them through a potato ricer.
2 Peel the garlic cloves and pound them in a pestle and mortar with the lemon juice. The second-best option is to use a hand blender for this process.
3 Mix the potato and the garlic together thoroughly in a bowl and then beat in the olive oil gradually with a wooden spoon. Beat in the whole egg. Season with salt and pepper, and remember that the taste of garlic will get stronger with time.

What goes with what ...
As well as being a fine addition to the mezedes table, this Skordalia recipe is an integral part of Fried Salt Cod.

lady's thighs

The traditional name for these elongated meatballs is the splendidly un-politically correct "lady's thighs" because of their shape. They work well as a cocktail snack or as part of a meze.

250g pie veal or lean beef

250g belly pork (ask your butcher to run the two meats through the mincer twice to mix them together thoroughly or use a food processor)

200g crustless white bread, soaked in milk and squeezed almost dry

2 bunches spring onions, finely chopped (include most of the green part)

1 dessertspoon finely chopped fresh flat-leaf parsley

1 dessertspoon fresh finely chopped mint

1 medium egg

1 teaspoon powdered cumin

1 teaspoon grated nutmeg

1 teaspoon powdered cinnamon

Sea salt and freshly ground black pepper

FOR FRYING

2 medium eggs

4 teaspoons milk

100g plain flour, seasoned with salt and pepper

100g fine breadcrumbs

Vegetable oil

1 In a bowl, knead the meat with the bread, spring onions, parsley and mint. Beat the egg in a cup and work it into the mixture, together with the cumin, nutmeg and cinnamon; season.

2 Use your hands to mould the mixture into pieces in the same shape as a lady's thigh and about 6cm long.

3 Beat the two eggs in a bowl with the milk to make an eggwash. Set out the seasoned flour and the breadcrumbs for coating on separate plates. Roll the "lady's thighs" in seasoned flour, then dip in the egg and finally, roll in the breadcrumbs.

4 In a fryer, heat the vegetable oil to approximately 170°C/340°F until hot, but not smoking. Fry the "lady's thighs" until cooked, about 4–5 minutes. Drain on kitchen paper.

What goes with what ...
These go well with Horta, Tzatziki or the oven-cooked beans (Gigandes Plaki). They should be eaten after they have cooled down a bit.

mock caviar salad

In the days when there was a substantial Greek population in Turkey (pre – 1926), the Caspian sea was full of sturgeon and the sturgeon were full of caviar. Back then, this recipe would have been made with genuine caviar. In these less bountiful times you can make it with black lumpfish roe and it will still taste very good. Should you ever get the urge to push the boat out and substitute real caviar for mock, it will taste even better.

25g black lumpfish roe
25g red lumpfish roe
25g crustless white bread, soaked in water and squeezed almost dry
1/2 a bunch spring onions, finely chopped
50ml olive oil
2 tablespoons freshly squeezed lemon juice
Sea salt and freshly ground black pepper

1 You cannot better an old-fashioned pestle and mortar for preparing this dish. If you do not have one, use your largest heaviest bowl and the back of a spoon. Put the caviar, bread and spring onions into the mortar and work them together.
2 Add the oil and lemon juice alternately, and gradually. When all is homogeneous, adjust the seasoning and serve cool but not chilled.

What goes with what ...
This dip provides a good counterpoint for a range of mezedes including Taramosalata, as shown, or as a topping for fresh oysters. Or just spread it thickly on plain, toasted sultana bread.

taramosalata

In its genuine incarnation this is a richly flavoured and satisfyingly dish, and to anyone accustomed to the pink, "industrial" version found in supermarkets, it will be something of a revelation. The original taramosalata used to be made with avgotaraho, the preserved roe of the grey mullet (much prized by the Italians, who know it as "bottarga"). However, soaring expense now dictates a cheaper alternative: salted cod's roe, or more usually smoked cod's roe, as the true salted roe can make the dish too salty for some tastes. You can also add a few finely chopped spring onions as a finishing touch, if you wish.

40g sliced white bread
200g smoked cod's roe
200ml olive oil
2 1/2 tablespoons freshly squeezed lemon juice
50ml warm water

1 Cut the crusts away from the bread and soak the slices briefly in water, then squeeze them until almost dry. Skin the cod's roe and break it up into chunks.
2 Put the bread and roe into a bowl and use a hand-held electric mixer to amalgamate them adding the oil gradually as you go. Start slowly, building up speed little by little. Add the lemon juice and warm water when most of the oil is incorporated as you go along. Alternatively, work the ingredients well with a wooden spoon. If the mixture is stiff, add a little more warm water.

What goes with what ...
Traditionally, this is only eaten once a year on "Clean Monday" (page 31), but it has become such an all-round meze that whatever it is served with, it will not let you down.

aubergines and courgettes in beer batter

This is an appetizer that is often served in Greece with a glass of wine or a cold beer.

Skordalia (page 34)
2 litres groundnut oil for frying
200g aubergines
200g courgettes
100g plain flour, very well
  seasoned

BATTER
200g white self-raising flour
330ml lager beer
Sea salt and freshly ground black
  pepper

1 Make the Skordalia, cover it and leave at room temperature to gain extra flavour if you are going to use it the same day.
2 To make the beer batter, whisk together the flour and beer. Season well, cover and put it to one side to improve for 1 hour.
3 Preheat your frying oil to 180°C/350°F.
4 Slice the aubergines and courgettes lengthways, about 3mm thick. Cover them in seasoned flour, then coat them in the batter. Before you drop them into the hot oil, hold them in the tongs so that all but the thinnest film of batter drains off. Then fry until golden, a few at a time so as to minimize the temperature drop in the oil.
5 Remove the battered vegetables from the oil and let them drain on kitchen paper for a few minutes until they are as dry as possible. Serve immediately, while they are still hot, with the Skordalia.

What goes with what ...
To make up a well-balanced selection of mezedes, this should be teamed with some Purée of Red Peppers with Feta, Dolmades, good feta and Cheese Triangles.

meat pastries

These baked meat pastries are the Greek version of spring rolls and this recipe comes from Cephalonia. If Captain Corelli ever enjoyed a snack, it would probably have been one of these.

50ml olive oil

200g shallots, peeled and chopped very finely (almost minced)

500g finely minced beef

100ml white wine

100ml homemade tomato sauce (or use passata)

1 dessertspoon finely chopped fresh flat-leaf parsley

2 dessertspoons finely chopped fresh mint

60g Greek feta cheese, crumbled

60g Kefalotiri cheese, grated (or substitute Pecorino)

2 medium eggs, lightly beaten

2 tablespoons breadcrumbs (on standby)

100g butter, melted

500g filo pastry

Sea salt and freshly ground black pepper

1 Preheat your oven to 180°C/350°F/Gas 4.

2 Heat the oil in a frying pan and fry the shallots until transparent. Add the minced beef and stir with a wooden spoon to separate and brown it all.

3 Add the wine and leave to simmer for 5–8 minutes. Stir in the tomato sauce, herbs and seasoning and leave to simmer for 20–25 minutes, stirring occasionally. Allow to cool.

4 Add the two cheeses and the egg (reserve some for eggwash), and if you think that the mixture is a bit runny, then stir in some breadcrumbs. Check the seasoning again and get ready to assemble the pastries.

5 Brush some melted butter onto half the width of each filo sheet. Fold the other half over the buttered part. Brush the plain surface with butter. Place 2 tablespoons of the filling in the centre of the pastry, about 2cm from the edge. Fold the two sides of filo sheet on top of the filling, brush again with butter and sprinkle with eggwash and roll up. Repeat the procedure until all mixture has been used up.

6 Arrange the pastries on a buttered baking sheet, then brush the tops with melted butter and eggwash. Bake for 45 to 60 minutes or until the tops are golden brown.

What goes with what ...
These are like tiny pasties and can be quite filling so they go well with plain yoghurt, Maroulosalata or Skordalia.

fagakia

THESE ARE DISHES WHICH WOULD PROBABLY BE CALLED STARTERS IN ANY

OTHER CUISINE. WHEN DINING IN GREECE, HOWEVER, THEY MAY ALSO

MAKE AN APPEARANCE ALONGSIDE THE MAIN COURSES AS "SIDE DISHES".

FOR THE HOME COOK THEY CAN BE EITHER STARTER, SUPPER DISH, LUNCH

OR MAIN COURSE. THEY ALL SERVE FOUR, UNLESS OTHERWISE STATED.

lahano dolmades με αυγολεμονο

The lahano cabbage is a vegetable that Greece shares with Turkey and the Middle East. Its large leaves soften when boiled, but retain their strength and this makes them perfect for large, meaty dolmades. This dish was one of our winter favourites and comes from the northern part of Greece. The recipe makes about 20 large dolmades.

200g minced beef

200g minced belly pork

200g Spanish onions, peeled and finely chopped

½ bunch of spring onions, finely chopped (including the green parts)

100g sultanas

4 tablespoons fresh flat-leaf parsley, finely chopped

1 whole flat-headed cabbage, preferably Lahano (or substitute the large, outer leaves from 4 heads of Cos lettuce or Chinese cabbage leaves)

1.5 litres chicken stock (you can use ready-made from supermarkets)

125g Greek short-grain or risotto rice

Sea salt and freshly ground black pepper

SAUCE

2 medium eggs, separated

6 teaspoons freshly squeezed lemon juice

1 tablespoon fresh, finely chopped dill

1 tablespoon fresh, finely chopped flat-leaf parsley

Sea salt and freshly ground black pepper

1 Combine the mince, Spanish onions, spring onions, sultanas and the parsley in a large bowl to make the filling. Mix them together thoroughly. Season and leave covered for 1 hour to allow the flavours to amalgamate.

2 Put the cabbage head in a large pot and fill with water. Place a couple of plates on top to ensure that it doesn't float, then cover and bring to the boil. Cook for 20–30 minutes until the cabbage is soft. Lift it out and transfer it to a large container of iced water. (If you cannot get Lahano and are substituting other leaves for the wrappers, strip off the largest outer leaves: the larger the better. Drop them into boiling water to blanch them then transfer to iced water. Proceed as for cabbage leaves, but you will have to be rather more careful as they are not so robust.)

3 Check the seasoning of the mince mixture by poaching a tablespoon-sized lump in a little chicken stock for 8 minutes, then taste it. Adjust the seasoning as necessary, mix in the rice and you are ready to make up the dolmades.

4 Roll each cabbage or lettuce leaf around a sausage shaped lump of filling. You are aiming for a finished parcel that is about 10cm long, although this will depend on the size of your wrapping leaves. As you complete each one, place them, join side down, in a pan with a lid and put a plate on top to keep them pressed down so that they do not unravel when cooking. Cover with the chicken stock and bring to the boil. Turn the heat down to a simmer and put the lid on. Cook for 45–60 minutes, until the rice is tender and has absorbed most of the stock. Allow the dolmades to cool down to lukewarm in the pan while you make the avgolemono sauce.

5 Quickly whisk the egg whites in a heatproof bowl until they form soft peaks. Then incorporate about 150ml of the chicken stock from the dolmades, then add the egg yolks a little at a time and finally the lemon juice, dill and parsley. Put the bowl over a pan of boiling water and continue stirring until the sauce thickens. Season to taste.

6 Drain the dolmades and serve lukewarm with the sauce.

φασολακια γιαχνι με παστουρμα
cannellini beans casseroled with pastourma

This is a dish that has its roots in Asia Minor. Hearty and warming, the one ingredient that may prove tricky to find is pastourma, which is a type of cured beef. Thankfully, it is now available in some British supermarkets and is relatively widespread in specialist Greek and Middle Eastern food shops. Pastourma is essentially a spicy, cured meat which was originally made from fillet of camel. It is now made from cured beef, rather like Bresaola, and it was probably the grandfather of the American smoked beef called Pastrami. The beef is cured with lots of sweet paprika and cumin.

500g cannellini beans
300g piece of pastourma
600ml beef or chicken stock
2.5 litres hot water
3 bunches of spring onions
1 bunch of fresh coriander, chopped
2 tablespoons butter
4 tablespoons extra virgin olive oil
Juice of 1 small lemon
1 teaspoon sugar
Sea salt
Flat bread, such as pitta, and mild green pickled chilli peppers to serve

1 Rinse the beans in fresh water and then soak them overnight. Rinse again and put them into a non-reactive saucepan.

2 Divide the pastourma into two pieces: one weighing 200g and the other 100g. Reserve the little piece and slice the larger one into four; put the pieces in with the beans. Add the stock and the water.

3 Bring to the boil and then simmer with the lid on until the beans are cooked, about 45–50 minutes. Take out the pastourma and discard. Chop the spring onions (including the green part) and add them to the casserole with the coriander.

4 Cut the remaining pastourma into strips for garnish and pan fry them briefly in the butter and 3 tablespoons oil. (They should take about 1 minute.) Keep an eye on them as they burn easily.

5 Add the pastourma strips, the frying pan juices, lemon juice, sugar and the remaining oil to the beans. Stir and season with salt to taste.

6 Serve this dish in deep bowls with some flat bread warmed under the grill and accompany it with some green chilli peppers.

μπαρμπουνια σαβορο
με μαυρες σταφιδες
cold soused red mullet with currants

This fish dish keeps well, which is important as it is traditionally made in advance for eating on the Sunday before Easter. The recipe comes from the island of Lefkada in the Ionian, where they serve it with a special Skordalia made with samphire.

1kg (about 3 or 4) large red mullet
   fillets (ask your fishmonger to
   remove the pin bones)
200ml olive oil
50g seasoned flour
Sea salt and freshly ground black
   pepper

MARINADE
1 litre extra virgin olive oil
300ml good-quality red wine
   vinegar
8 cloves of garlic, peeled and
   thinly sliced
200g currants
5 sprigs of fresh rosemary (about
   2cm long)

1 Season the fish fillets and put them to one side at room temperature for 20 minutes.

2 Heat the ordinary olive oil in a large frying pan. Roll the fillets in the seasoned flour and shallow-fry them. Cook them for 2 minutes on each side, which means that the centre will be slightly undercooked. Remove them with a slotted spoon and let them cool down completely on a rack.

3 Put the extra virgin olive oil, vinegar, garlic, currants and rosemary in a saucepan and bring to simmering point. Cover and cook for 10 minutes until the currants and garlic are soft, then check the seasoning of the marinade.

4 Take a container with a lid that is suitable for the fridge and sprinkle a few of the currants over the bottom. Add a layer of red mullet, then pour over enough of the hot marinade to cover the first layer of fish. Continue doing the same until you've used up all the ingredients: the final top layer should be the currants and the marinade should be used to cover everything. When the marinade has settled down, the olive oil should form an unbroken film over the surface and this will protect the fish.

5 Leave in the fridge for 1 week before eating. Serve at room temperature.

σπαγγετι με αυγοταραχο
pasta with avgotaraho

The Italians stole dried mullet roe from the Greeks, who call it avgotaraho. Italian restaurants and modernist Italian chefs make much of bottarga (grey mullet) and charge accordingly. We were using avgotaraho centuries ago, and it tastes so much better. So saying, this recipe will also work with bottarga or even the humble smoked cod's roe (avgotaraho is hard to find), and Italian pasta will do fine.

500g macaroni or tagliatelle

a little olive oil

30g butter

80g avgotaraho (remove the wax and place in the freezer for 30 minutes before use)

3 tablespoons finely chopped fresh chervil

sea salt

DRESSING

150ml extra virgin olive oil

$^1/_2$ the juice and zest of 1 lemon

$^1/_2$ the juice and zest of 1 orange

2 cloves of garlic, peeled and crushed (if you are preparing this dish during the months of March or April, use ramsons – fresh green garlic leaves – instead)

Sea salt and freshly ground black pepper

warm salad of mixed greens, to serve

1 Cook the pasta in plenty of boiling water with some salt and a drizzle of olive oil according to the directions on the packet. While the pasta is boiling, make the dressing by mixing together the extra virgin olive oil, lemon and orange zest and juice, and the garlic in a bowl. Season well.

2 When the pasta is ready, drain it through a sieve. Put the cold knob of butter in the same pot and melt it over high heat to release its aroma and flavour. Toss the drained pasta in it until coated. Empty the pasta into a large bowl and pour over the olive oil dressing. Mix thoroughly once again.

3 Grate the avgotaraho over the hot pasta, add the chopped chervil and toss together again.

4 This dish works well served with a warm salad of mixed greens.

aubergine roulades

This recipe and the Onion-Boiled Eggs (page 16) are from the Jewish community in Thessalonki, which explains why they are served together. As is usually the case with Greek cuisine, this recipe combines vegetables with meat and a sauce, making it a very well balanced dish.

1.5kg large aubergines
500ml groundnut oil for frying

STUFFING
500g beef mince
100g Spanish onions, peeled and
    finely chopped
50g white, crustless bread
2 tablespoons finely chopped
    fresh mint
Sea salt and freshly ground black
    pepper

SAUCE
1kg plum tomatoes
2 small, hot red chilli peppers
1 green pepper
125ml olive oil
Sea salt and freshly ground black
    pepper

1 Put all the ingredients for the stuffing in a large mixing bowl and mix together well. Leave to rest, covered, for 1 hour at room temperature to let the flavours amalgamate.

2 Preheat your oven to 200°C/400°F/Gas 6. Slice the aubergines lengthways and very thinly (use a mandolin if you have one), and shallow-fry them briefly in the groundnut oil until soft. Remove and place on kitchen paper to absorb any excess oil.

3 To make the sauce, remove the skins, then deseed and finely chop the plum tomatoes. Deseed and finely chop the red chilli peppers and green pepper. Heat the olive oil in a frying pan and add the tomatoes, chillies and peppers. Season and cook until you've got a sauce, which will take about 30 minutes. Adjust the seasoning if necessary.

4 To prepare the dish, take a roasting tray of about 25 x 25 x 5cm and spread a little of the tomato sauce over the bottom. Then take a walnut sized piece of the stuffing and a slice of aubergine. Put the stuffing at one end of the aubergine and roll it up. Continue in this way until you have used up all the aubergines and stuffing.

5 Place the little aubergine roulades, flap side down to stop them unrolling, on top of the tomato sauce in the roasting tray. Pour over the remaining tomato sauce and bake for about 1 hour until thoroughly cooked.

kiofte within kiofte

This dish comes from Capadoccia in Asia Minor. It was traditionally made for 6th January, which is when the Greek Orthdox church goes to bless the waters. Folklore has it that the men of Capadoccia would visit Ismir just before Christmas to buy the Seville oranges needed for the tangy dressing; for the rest of the year they, like us, would make do with lemon juice. The filling (Inner Kiofte) needs to be made in advance as it needs extra time to chill down.

2.5 litres homemade beef stock (page 181) or use ready made supermarket stock

125ml extra virgin olive oil

juice of 1 Seville orange (or substitute lemon)

Sea salt and freshly ground black pepper

INNER KIOFTE

30g butter

6 teaspoons olive oil

500g Spanish onions, peeled and finely chopped

500g fine beef mince

500g fine pork mince

1 tablespoon cumin seeds, dry roasted in a frying pan and then roughly ground

1 dessertspoon freshly ground nutmeg

1/4 teaspoon cayenne pepper

100ml water

Sea salt and freshly ground black pepper

OUTER KIOFTE

500g very fine bulgar wheat

250g fine beef mince

1 pinch of cayenne pepper

3 medium eggs

140g (approximately) plain flour

Sea salt and freshly ground black pepper

1 To make the inner kiofte, put the butter and olive oil in a frying pan and sauté the chopped onions for 3–4 minutes.

2 Add both lots of mince and brown them quickly.

3 Now add the cumin, nutmeg, cayenne pepper and seasoning; stir well. Stir in the water and cook until you've got no water left and the mince is cooked. (It should be light and separate.) Let the mixture cool down and then cover and refrigerate for 24 hours or overnight.

4 Soak the bulgar wheat for the outer kiofte in a little water until it starts to soften but be very careful not to overwet it. When it is soft, place it in a large mixing bowl with the rest of the outer kiofte ingredients and mix together thoroughly. Add the flour gradually, keep mixing the ingredients together and the final result should be a kneadable mixture.

5 You are now ready to assemble the kiofte. The key is to work with wet hands. Take a piece of the outer mix about the size of an egg and make a hole in the middle. Then take a smaller piece of the cold "inner" mixture and use it as a stuffing by moulding the outer layer around it until until you have a meatball.

6 To cook the meatballs, take a large pot and fill it with stock. Bring the stock to boiling point, season it and drop in the stuffed kiofte. When they float to the surface they are ready.

7 Arrange the kiofte in a serving bowl and drizzle with a simple dressing of extra virgin olive oil and citrus juice.

πιτουλα με ρυζι και τυρακι
yoghurt, rice and feta pie

This is one of my father's favourites: an excellent, rich dish from Epirus. Try it with a Salad of Green Peppers and Peaches (page 118) or the Maroulosalata (page 123). Ready made filo won't do the job here as it's already too thinly rolled. Instead, spend 10 minutes following the recipe for the homemade filo.

2 teaspoons butter (for greasing the tin)
500g homemade filo (page 132)
Plain flour for rolling out
600ml whole milk
1 tablespoon olive oil
300g Greek short-grain risotto rice
300g good-quality Greek yoghurt (or substitute another thick yoghurt)
350g feta cheese
1 bunch of spring onions, very finely chopped
40g dill, finely chopped
4 medium eggs
water or milk for sealing
sesame seeds for sprinkling
Sea salt and freshly ground black pepper

1 Grease a 20cm loose-bottomed or spring-release cake tin. Divide the filo dough into two unequal pieces of 300g and 200g. On a floured surface, roll out the larger piece of pastry to a circle of about 30cm across. Cover the base of the tin with it. Roll out a second pastry piece large enough to cover the top of the tin. Wrap both bits of pastry in damp tea towels and put in the fridge to rest while you work on the filling.

2 Preheat your oven to 180°C/350°F/Gas 4.

3 Put the milk, olive oil and a pinch of salt in a large, heavy-bottomed saucepan and bring to the boil. Add the rice and stir well, then cover and leave to simmer for approximately 20 minutes.

4 In the meantime, put the yoghurt and feta cheese in a food processor and work it until you've got a smooth paste. Add the spring onions and dill, and let the processor run for just 2 seconds.

5 Use the processor on pulse to add three of the eggs, one at a time. (Allow each one to be incorporated before you add the next.)

6 Add the egg mixture to the cooked rice. Stir to mix thoroughly and place in the prepared pastry case. With a palette knife, smooth the top and cover with the second piece of pastry. Moisten the edges with lukewarm water or milk, seal well and crimp the edges if you like pretty-looking pies.

7 In a bowl, beat the last egg to make an egg wash and glaze the top of the pie. Sprinkle with sesame seeds and bake for 1 hour to 1 hour 10 minutes.

8 Allow the pie to cool down until lukewarm before eating; it will then be at its best. If your greed deprives you of the patience to wait until it is lukewarm, you must allow a minimum of 20 minutes!

imam bayaldi

Versions of this dish have become something of a favourite with fashionable chefs. We Greeks have been enjoying it for years, which only goes to show just how closely aligned the cuisines of the Eastern Mediterranean can be.

1.5kg large aubergines (at least 12cm long, if possible and the thin ones rather than the fat kind)

1.3kg Spanish onions, peeled and thinly sliced

100ml olive oil

1 dessertspoon sugar

200g plum tomatoes, peeled, deseeded and chopped

2 nutmegs grated

4 heaped tablespoons finely chopped flat-leaf parsley

100ml water

5 cloves of garlic, peeled and thinly sliced

Sea salt and freshly ground black pepper

1 Peel half the skin away from the aubergines in long strips so that they look stripy. With the tip of a paring knife, make a deep slash lengthways on each aubergine. Sprinkle them with salt and allow them to stand for 30 minutes, then rinse.

2 Preheat your oven to 180°C/350°F/Gas 4.

3 Put the onions into a frying pan with 50ml of the olive oil and the sugar. Cook very slowly for about 1 hour until they are completely soft, like a light brown jam.

4 Take a third of the mixture and spread it over the base of an oiled casserole. Then add a layer of chopped tomatoes and put to one side.

5 Add the remaining tomatoes to the fried onions in the frying pan; also the nutmeg and half the parsley. Mix well and cook for 10 minutes.

6 Add the water to the frying pan contents and stir. Arrange the aubergines on the onion mixture in the bottom of the casserole and with a spoon, stuff the garlic slices into the slashes in the aubergines. Then add the frying pan contents to the casserole and try to work it into the slashes in the aubergines as well. The casserole should be overflowing!

7 Season well and pour the remaining oil over the contents. Cover the casserole with a sheet of foil and then put the lid on. This should ensure a good seal.

8 Cook in the oven for 40 minutes or until the aubergines are really soft. If you like a thick sauce, remove the lid for the last 10 minutes to allow it to dry off a little.

9 Allow to cool until it is lukewarm, then sprinkle with the remaining parsley and serve.

φακες
lentil soup

No matter how big your dining table, you will always run out of space when you want to serve this soup. Traditionally, it serves as a backdrop to all sorts of additional flavours – lakerda, olives, salty, pan fried cheese, anchovies and capers. My mother always used to cook this dish on Wednesday, so for us Tuesday night meant a long session sorting through the lentils by hand to get rid of the stones. She used to check our work by throwing handfuls of the lentils into a metal bowl and would listen out for the chink that meant a tiny pebble.

500g small green lentils
250g whole, peeled shallots
3 cloves of garlic, peeled, and left whole
4 bay leaves
3 litres water
200ml extra virgin olive oil
40ml red wine vinegar to serve
Sea salt and freshly ground black pepper

1 Put the lentils, shallots, garlic and bay leaves into a large pot and add the water. Place the pot over a medium heat and let it come to a simmer. Leave to simmer, uncovered, for 2$\frac{1}{2}$ hours. Skim regularly for the first 20 minutes, then stir in 100ml of the olive oil. Season at the last minute.

2 Divide the soup between 4 bowls and drizzle the remaining olive oil equally between bowls. Add a little vinegar to each bowl and serve.

χταποδι στην σχαρα
grilled octopus

This dish could be either fagakia or meze depending on how much of it you wish to serve. It comes from the Greek islands and is one of those small dishes that goes down well during the hot days when you haven't got much appetite, or as a snack after a day on the beach.

500g octopus (try and get the one with a double line of suckers and ask your fishmonger to prepare it)

DRESSING
Juice of 1 lemon
1 dessertspoon made mustard
40ml extra virgin olive oil
1 heaped tablespoon finely chopped fresh thyme
Freshly ground black pepper

1 Put a rack in a roasting tray and sit the octopus upon it. Preheat your oven to its lowest possible temperature and leave the octopus in it for 3–4 hours. The objective is to dry the octopus out, and a surprising amount of water will accumulate in the tray.

2 Cut the octopus into manageable chunks and cook it under a hot grill for 10–15 minutes. (In the summer it can go straight onto the barbecue.)

3 Meanwhile, prepare the dressing. In a bowl, mix together the lemon juice and mustard, and then work in the olive oil bit by bit until you have a thick and cloudy dressing. Adjust to taste with the thyme and some freshly ground black pepper.

4 Dress the grilled octopus with the dressing and serve.

κοτοσουπα αυγολεμονο
chicken avgolemono soup

Jewish mothers don't have the monopoly on the medicinal properties of chicken soup. The slightest hint of a winter cold has Greek matriarchs dishing out nutritious chicken soup to all and sundry. This dish also has a legendary reputation as a hangover cure.

1kg carrots, peeled and left whole

3 bay leaves

1 large (1.5kg) chicken

1kg leeks, washed, trimmed of green parts (cut in half horizontally, if very long).

2 bunches of spring onions, trimmed, washed and left whole

100g Greek short-grain rice or risotto rice

2 medium eggs, separated

Juice of 2 lemons

50g butter

Sea salt and freshly ground black pepper

1 Put about 2 litres water into a large pot and add the carrots and bay leaves. Bring to boiling point and cook for 10 minutes.

2 Turn the heat down and submerge the whole chicken. Leave to simmer with the lid on for 30 minutes.

3 Add the leeks and spring onions, and keep simmering for a further 15 minutes.

4 Remove the cooked chicken and the vegetables with a slotted spoon and keep them warm. Carve the chicken into portions and cut up the vegetables.

5 Add the rice to the broth, of which there should be about 1.5 litres, and stir to prevent the rice sticking. Leave to simmer for 10 minutes, or until the rice is barely cooked.

6 To finish thickening the soup, first whisk the egg whites until they peak in a mixing bowl. Add a quarter of the broth to the bowl, a little at a time and fold in, together with the lemon juice and finally, the egg yolks.

7 Reduce the heat under the soup to a minimum (some people transfer everything to a bain-marie at this point) and stir the contents of the mixing bowl back into the bulk of the soup. Keep stirring until the soup thickens. On no account let the soup boil or it will curdle. Season with salt and pepper.

8 Float a knob of butter in each bowl of soup as you serve it. It can be eaten either alongside the chicken and vegetables, or on its own as a first course. The chicken and vegetables should be eaten at room temperature.

gigandes plaki

The key to this dish is to start off with good beans. In Greek shops you may find the beans called Gigandes, which is why the dish is called Gigandes Plaki. The best beans come from Macedonia and Epirus, and the new season's supply arrives in the shops in the autumn. They are sweeter and less tough than those which have been sitting around since the year before.

500g Gigandes beans

2 red onions, peeled and finely chopped

3 cloves of garlic, peeled and finely sliced

80–100ml olive oil

150g fresh plum tomatoes, peeled, deseeded and diced

1 carrot, peeled and chopped

2 stalks of celery (including any leaves), chopped

2 bay leaves

1 tablespoon fresh thyme leaves.

2 tablespoons flat-leaf parsley, chopped

Sea salt and freshly ground black pepper

1 Wash the beans and soak overnight in a bowl of cold water. The next day, bring to the boil and then discard the soaking water. Cover the beans again in fresh water and simmer with the lid on until the beans become just tender.

2 Preheat your oven to170°C/325°F/Gas 3.

3 Sauté the onions and garlic in the oil until soft. Add the plum tomatoes, carrot and celery. Cook for about 10 minutes, then use a hand blender to purée the vegetables.

4 Put the vegetable mixture and the beans into a flat dish (this will help ensure they cook evenly) and stir together. Add the bay leaves and the thyme. Season to taste with salt and pepper. Cook in the oven for 1^{1}/$_{2}$–2 hours, or until the beans are tender and almost all the liquid has been absorbed. Look at the dish occasionally and if more liquid is needed, add a little hot water from a kettle. On no account add cold water as it will make the skins of the beans tough.

5 Add the chopped parsley and stir well before serving. Eat the gigandes at room temperature: if you chill them, the olive oil may "split" out of the sauce.

πρασα με ντοματα
leeks stewed with tomatoes and prunes

An Eastern combination of flavours, this dish either works as an original vegetarian meal or as the perfect partner for any plainly grilled meat or fish. The recipe comes from Constantinople, which used to be the centre of the world trade in dried fruit. Greeks have long suspected that the French traders buying a year's supply of fruit were also stealing all the best recipes, which is why French cuisine is what it is today.

1kg small leeks, washed and trimmed

500g plum tomatoes, skinned, deseeded, and roughly chopped

400ml chicken stock

1 bunch of spring onions, chopped into 2cm lengths (including most of the green part)

1 stalk of celery and a few of the leafy bits, chopped

300g no-need-to-soak pitted prunes

1 level tablespoon finely chopped flat-leaf parsley

Leaves from 2 sprigs of fresh thyme

2 tablespoons butter

2 tablespoons olive oil

2 tablespoons lemon juice

Sea salt and freshly ground black pepper

1 Cut the leeks into 3cm pieces and soak them in hand-hot water for about 10 minutes, which will reduce their "oniony" taste. Drain them and throw the water away.

2 Take a heavy saucepan and add the tomatoes, leeks, chicken stock, spring onions, celery, prunes, parsley, thyme, butter and oil. Mix together gently.

3 Season with salt and pepper, and simmer, uncovered, until all is tender – about 20–30 minutes. For the first 10 minutes, skim with a spoon occasionally to remove any scum that has risen to the surface. When ready, add the lemon juice.

fish soup
κακαβια

The best fish soup is eaten on the fishing boats, because, on the leeside of the boat, out of the wind there is always a stockpot bubbling away. As the fishermen haul in the nets, this is where all the very small fish end up. Once the stock is prepared, remember that it is most important to continue to skim throughout the final cooking.

Fish stock (see next page)
1/2g saffron (leave to soak somewhere warm in 2 tablespoons white wine)
75g plum tomatoes, peeled, seeded and diced
150g small carrots, peeled and left whole

1 Before you begin to make the stock, all the whole fish must be gutted, gilled, bloodless and rinsed very well. The fish bones, too, must be bloodless and well rinsed. (Your fishmonger can do this for you.)
2 Put the fish and bones into a large stockpot or casserole, and add approximately a quarter of the weight of fish in vegetables. Top up with enough water to cover everything.
3 Bring to the boil, then turn the heat down. Start skimming and leave to simmer until stock is tasty, but remains light and not too fishy, about 45 minutes to 1 hour.

150g small leeks, trimmed, washed and left whole

100g small new potatoes, washed

4 stalks of celery, trimmed and peeled, then cut into 8cm lengths

1kg lobster (use the claws and the tail)

750g filleted white fish – cod, brill and John Dory are all fine

75g crevettes (left whole)

40g Greek short-grain or risotto rice, rinsed for 5 minutes

1 tablespoon finely chopped flat-leaf parsley, including the stalks

1 dessertspoon finely chopped dill weed, including the stalks

4 teaspoons celery leaves

Juice of 1 lemon

50ml extra virgin olive oil

Sea salt and freshly ground black pepper

STOCK

250g gurnard (or substitute cod trimmings)

250g red mullet

Fish bones from fish such as brill, turbot, monkfish, conger eel, lemon or Dover sole and John Dory

Trimmings from vegetables such as carrots, leeks, onions, garlic, tomatoes, stalks of parsley or dill and celery leaves

4 Pass the stock through a sieve into another container, while you wash out the pot. Then put the stock back in the pan.

5 Bring the prepared stock to the boil and add the saffron, plum tomatoes and carrots. Leave to simmer for 10 minutes.

6 Add the leeks and potatoes, and cook for a further 12 minutes Then add the celery and cook for 10 more minutes .

7 Add the lobster tail and claws to the soup and 5 minutes later add the brill, John Dory, cod and crevettes. Leave to simmer for 5 more minutes.

8 With a perforated spatula, remove the fish and vegetables. Place on a serving dish. Add the rice to the pot, cook for 10 minutes and then add the herbs, celery leaves, half the lemon juice, half the olive oil and adjust the seasoning to your taste.

9 The fish and vegetables should be dressed with ladolemono (simply mix the remaining lemon juice and olive oil) and the soup should be eaten hot with plenty of crusty bread and pickled vegetables.

γεμιστα βερυκοκα και δαμασκηνα

dried fruits stuffed with savoury minced meat

This is a genuine fagakia, but it can stand on its own as a starter and is also an excellent snack served with cocktails. The mix of flavours is typical of Eastern Greece.

300ml water

1 x 5cm stick of cinnamon

3 cloves

75g butter

1 red onion, peeled and finely diced

1 bunch of spring onions, finely chopped (including most of the green part)

400g finely ground minced veal

1 tablespoon finely chopped fresh mint

1 teaspoon sugar

350g large "no-need-to-soak" dried apricots, pitted

350g large "no-need-to-soak" dried prunes, pitted

Sea salt and freshly ground black pepper

rice pilaffs, to serve

1 Put the water in a non-reactive saucepan and add the cinnamon and the cloves. Bring to the boil, put the lid on and turn down the heat. Simmer for 30 minutes, then strain into a jug. Cover and set aside.

2 Heat 2 tablespoons of the butter in a frying pan and fry the red onion and spring onions until soft. Stir the mince into the vegetables, being careful to break up any lumps. Cook for a further 5 minutes over a medium heat with the lid on.

3 Preheat your oven to 180°C/350°F/Gas 4.

4 Add the flavoured water to the mince mixture and continue to cook, uncovered, for about 20 minutes. Then add the mint and sugar. Season to taste with salt and pepper.

5 Slice each of the dried fruits open and use a piping bag (or a tiny teaspoon) to fill each one with the veal mince. Stand them upright in a flat greased ovenproof dish. Melt the remaining butter and drizzle it over the fruits. Bake in the oven for 30 minutes.

6 Serve the fruits hot or at room temperature with a simple rice pilaff. Garnish with plenty of fresh mint and serve yoghurt with fresh mint chopped into it as an accompaniment, perhaps with a very light dusting of red pepper.

"The discovery of a new dish is more valuable to humanity than the discovery of a new star"

thracian sausages

Making sausages is a fairly daunting task and one that is made a good deal easier if you happen to have one of those food mixers that has a sausage-making attachment. If you do not have this gadget, do not despair: simply use a piping bag. It will work just as well, despite being a touch more messy. This recipe originated in Thraki. The sausages will keep for up to two days in the fridge and should be rested for at least six hours before cooking. This recipe makes about 1kg of sausages.

150g leeks, trimmed and very finely chopped

1 medium Spanish onion, peeled and finely chopped

100ml olive oil

200g finely minced pork (enlist the help of your butcher)

100g finely minced, smoked streaky bacon

100g pig's liver, finely minced

1 pig's kidney, finely minced (or use skinned lambs kidneys with the fat removed)

2 heaped tablespoons Hungarian sweet paprika

250g passata

2 tablespoons finely chopped, fresh flat-leaf parsley

100g fine bulgur wheat

1 dessertspoon sea salt and 8 twists of freshly ground black pepper

2 metres sausage skins (ask your butcher)

Juice of 1 lemon

1 In a large frying pan, sweat the leeks and the onion together in 50ml olive oil until soft.

2 Tip the leeks and onions into a large bowl and add the pork, bacon, liver, kidney and paprika. Mix together well. Return the mixture to the pan and cook until it takes on a little colour.

3 Again, using a mixing bowl add the passata, parsley and bulgur wheat. Mix together well, then taste and adjust the seasoning. Leave to stand until the wheat has absorbed all the liquid, about 30 minutes.

4 Fill the sausage skins loosely with the mixture. If you overfill them, they will split when cooked and you are aiming for a thinner, chipolata kind of sausage. (If you are unable to find sausage skins, you can form the mixture into rounds, cover them sparingly with breadcrumbs and fry them in the remaining olive oil before adding the lemon juice rather than following the poaching instructions below.)

5 To cook the sausages, simply cover the bottom of your pan with 2cm of water. Add the remaining olive oil and lemon juice, and then poach the sausages gently. The water will eventually evaporate and the sausages will brown in the oil.

φρεσκα πρασινα
φασολακια με πατατουλες
απο τον μορια

green beans,
new potatoes and herbs

This is a dish from the Peloponnese. Let the food cool down and serve it with plenty of feta cheese and bread for dipping in the sauce. During the hot days of the summer this dish is eaten at room temperature and it improves with keeping. On the second day, it will taste even better.

2 bunches of spring onions,
    trimmed and roughly chopped
100ml olive oil
250g plum tomatoes peeled,
    deseeded and roughly chopped
    (or substitute 250ml passata)
500g French beans, trimmed and
    cut in half (you can substitute
    runner beans, but must
    remember to remove the
    strings from their sides and cut
    them into 4cm lengths)
1 dessertspoon finely chopped
    fresh flat-leaf parsley
2 dessertspoons finely chopped
    fresh mint
150g new potatoes, peeled and
    left whole
40ml extra virgin olive oil
Sea salt and freshly ground black
    pepper

1 Take a large saucepan and sweat the spring onions in the olive oil for 3 or 4 minutes, or until they are softened.

2 Add the fresh tomatoes or passata, cook for a further 5 minutes and then add the green beans, chopped parsley and mint, and enough water to almost cover. Tuck the new potatoes in between the green beans, season and cover the pan. Leave to simmer for 30 minutes.

3 Check the seasoning and cook, uncovered, until the vegetables are done, about 20 more minutes.

4 Let everything cool down. Drizzle with the extra virgin olive oil and serve at room temperature.

white fish terrine

τσιλαδια ή πηχτη απο ψαρι

This dish is typical wedding fare. A Greek wedding buffet would not be complete without fish terrine. It was also a favourite dish of my mother and she used to make it when we had large family parties.

JELLY

40ml olive oil

100g carrots, roughly chopped

50g Spanish onions, peeled and
   roughly chopped

50g celery, roughly chopped

1kg conger eel (ask your
   fishmonger for the head)

Brill bones (ask your fishmonger
   for the trimmings, see below)

90ml white wine

Sea salt and freshly ground black
   pepper

1 To prepare the jelly, place the olive oil, carrots, onions, celery, conger eel and the brill bones in a large, heavy pot. Sauté quickly and do not let them colour.

2 Deglaze the pot with the white wine and scrape away any bits stuck to the bottom. Add enough water to just cover the fish and vegetables, season, bring to the boil and allow to simmer for 45 minutes to 1 hour to produce a stock.

3 For the terrine, season the brill fillets. Mix the olive oil with the white wine vinegar in a bowl and rub it into the fillets. Leave to marinate in a bowl until it is needed.

4 Pass the fish stock through a colander and then through muslin into a clean pot. Bring it back to simmering point and add the diced carrots, leeks, celery and the saffron infusion.

TERRINE

500g brill fillets, the thicker the
  better (remember to ask for the
  trimmings)
25ml olive oil
25ml white wine vinegar
50g carrots, finely diced
100g leeks, finely diced
40g celery, peeled and cut into
  4cm long pieces
$\frac{1}{3}$g saffron (put it in a glass with
  75ml white wine and allow to
  infuse somewhere warm)
1 tablespoon celery leaves, finely
  shredded
1 tablespoon flowery fennel tops
Sea salt and freshly ground black
  pepper

PICKLED VEGETABLE
MAYONNAISE

1 dessertspoon white wine
  vinegar
1 dessertspoon Dijon mustard
Yolk of 1 medium egg
40ml olive oil and 40ml
  good-quality vegetable oil,
  mixed together
1 dessertspoon lemon juice
200g pickled vegetables
Sea salt and freshly ground black
  pepper

5 Cook until the vegetables are done, but still crunchy. Add the brill fillets and take the pot off the heat. Allow the fish to poach gently in the cooling liquid. When cool, remove the fish and vegetables from the stock and if you have more than 350ml of liquid, boil down to reduce to that amount.

6 Take a terrine dish or bowl and put about 6 teaspoons of the liquid into the bottom. Cover and refrigerate for a few hours until set.

7 To make the pickled vegetable mayonnaise, put the vinegar in a mixing bowl. Dissolve the mustard in the vinegar. Add the egg yolk and with an electric hand mixer, start whisking until the mayonnaise is thick enough to coat the beater.

8 Begin to add the mixture of olive and vegetable oil in droplets, increasing very gradually as the sauce thickens. Slowly add the lemon juice and oil alternately and beat steadily. Adjust the seasoning.

9 Finely chop the pickled vegetables and add them to the mayonnaise.

10 Build the terrine up in layers, setting each one in the refrigerator as you go along. First the fish, then the stock and then the pickled vegetable mayonnaise. Then the stock and then the fish, followed by the celery leaves and fennel tops; then stock, vegetables and fish until you have filled the terrine. Finally, refrigerate until firm. To serve, cut into slices with a hot knife.

stuffed mussels

Use the large mussels, which are sometimes known rather unflatteringly as horse mussels, for this dish. You will find that they are a good deal easier to stuff than the smaller ones.

20 large mussels (or 40 small ones)

15g pine kernels

100ml olive oil

½ bunch of spring onions, finely chopped (including most of the green part)

1 medium Spanish onion, peeled and very finely chopped

50g risotto rice or Greek short-grain rice

Juice of ½ a lemon

2 teaspoons sultanas

½ tablespoon caster sugar

½ teaspoon powdered cumin

¼ teaspoon cayenne pepper

1 teaspoon powdered cinnamon

100ml water

Sea salt

1 Wash the mussels and remove the parts that my mother describes as "their moustaches".

2 Dry-roast the pine kernels in a heavy pan until they are golden brown. Add 50ml olive oil, the spring onions and the Spanish onion. Sauté for 5 minutes.

3 Add the rice, lemon juice, sultanas, sugar, cumin, cayenne and cinnamon to the pan. Mix together thoroughly, then remove the pan from the heat and allow to cool. Add salt to taste.

4 With a small, sharp knife, open the mussels carefully. Don't overdo it, or they will tear. Stuff each mussel with 2 teaspoons of the mixture and keep them shut by wrapping them with string. Black string looks better, but it can be hard to find.

5 Place the mussels in a heavy pot and add the remaining olive oil and the water. Cover it and cook gently until all the liquid is absorbed. This may take about 30–40 minutes. Allow to cool and serve the dish at room temperature.

φασολαδα
cannellini bean soup

Fassolada (cannellini bean soup) is the nearest thing that anyone can agree on as being a Greek national dish and it has a very ancient provenance. The Greek proverb about patience is "fassouli to fassouli yemizi to sakouli" (bean by bean, the sack is filled).

400g cannellini beans, soaked for
   24 hours
4 bay leaves
200g mild onions, peeled and
   finely chopped,
100g carrots, peeled and finely
   diced
3 stalks of celery (including any
   leaves), finely chopped (reserve
   the leaves separately)
150g ripe plum tomatoes,
   deseeded, skinned and diced
125ml extra virgin olive oil
4 heaped tablespoons finely
   chopped flat-leaf parsley
Sea salt and freshly ground black
   pepper

1 Drain the beans from the soaking water. Put them in a large pan and add 5 litres water and the bay leaves. Bring to the boil and cook for 1 1/2 hours.
2 Turn the heat down and add the onions, carrots, celery stalks and cook, uncovered, for 1 hour.
3 Add the tomatoes, season to taste and half the olive oil. Cook for 30 minutes more, or until the beans are very tender.
4 Remove from the heat and season to taste. Pour into bowls and drizzle with some of the remaining olive oil to serve. Sprinkle a share of the chopped herbs over each bowl and garnish with celery leaves.

cold fish with vegetables and mayonnaise

This is the kind of dish that the Victorians would probably have described as a "savoury mould" and it would be served as a starter at a smart dinner party or as an original accompaniment to hot fish soup. Each diner gets a small mound of fish and vegetables loosely bound together with mayonnaise. Start with good-quality fish and the dish will end up surprisingly sophisticated. This dish serves 8.

500g large, uncooked prawns (the ones known as crevettes)

50ml olive oil

1 x 1kg Dover sole (ask your fishmonger to fillet it and keep the bones to make stock)

1 x 1kg red mullet (again, ask your fishmonger to fillet it and for the bones for stock)

500g small leeks (including the white parts), trimmed and washed

500g carrots, peeled and diced

6 celery stalks, peeled

4 bay leaves

250ml white wine

250g potatoes, peeled and diced

2 bunches of spring onions, trimmed and cut into 3cm lengths

Juice of 1 lemon

4 heaped tablespoons roughly chopped flat-leaf parsley

2 heaped tablespoons chopped fresh dill

100g caper berries

150g pickled vegetables (cauliflower, carrots and gherkins)

MAYONNAISE

2 medium egg yolks

1 teaspoon dry English mustard

250ml olive oil

Juice of 1 small lemon

40ml chilled fish stock (see method)

Sea salt and freshly ground black pepper

1 Peel the prawns and put them to one side. Add the shells to a big pot, together with the olive oil.

2 Wash the fish bones and add them to the pot. Chop half the leeks and add them to the pot, together with half the carrots, half the celery and the bay leaves.

3 Sweat everything over a medium heat until the vegetables are getting soft, but not too brown. Add the white wine and stir to release any bits that stick to the base. Add enough water to cover everything and bring back to the boil. Lower the heat and leave to simmer, uncovered, for 30 minutes. Strain the stock through muslin and return it to the pot.

4 Put the pot back over a medium heat and add the diced potatoes, the remaining carrots and celery, the whole leeks and spring onions. Cook for about 20 minutes or until the vegetables are soft. Remove the vegetables from the stock and set aside to cool down.

5 Add the lemon juice and 2 tablespoons of flat-leaf parsley to the stock. Bring it back to simmering point and poach the fillets of sole and red mullet for 6–8 minutes. Remove and set aside to drain and cool. Poach the prawns for 3 or 4 minutes, remove and set aside to cool. Return the stock to the heat and boil until it has reduced to about 100ml. Add the chopped dill and place in the fridge to set.

6 Make the mayonnaise by beating the egg yolks in a bowl, together with the mustard. Work the oil in gradually and then thin the mix down with the lemon juice. Add the cold fish stock and season to taste.

7 To serve, flake the fish into a large mixing bowl and add the prawns, the cooked vegetables, caper berries and pickled vegetables. Bind together with the mayonnaise. Check the seasoning.

8 Line eight large (10cm) dariole moulds (or small bowls) with cling film. Place a whole prawn in each one first so that it is on top when you turn them out, then pack with the vegetable mixture. Cover and refrigerate for at least 1 hour and then use the cling film to ease them out onto a plate so that each one looks like a small dome.

main dishes

THE FOLLOWING ARE MAIN DISHES – LARGER, MORE SUBSTANTIAL DISHES

THAT PROVIDE A BALANCE OF TASTES AND TEXTURES IN THEMSELVES.

UNLESS OTHERWISE STATED THEY SERVE FOUR PEOPLE.

okra baked with tomatoes and parsley

My mother could never explain to me just what chemical reaction happened when she dropped the okra into the white vinegar, but the vinegar certainly gets rid of its gluey substance. This is very good at room temperature and, as with all our summer dishes, it tastes better the next day. You can keep it in the fridge for up to three days.

1kg okra
300ml white wine vinegar
250g shallots, peeled and thinly cut lengthways
150g green peppers, split, cored and deseeded, then thinly cut lengthways into strips
500g ripe plum tomatoes, peeled, deseeded and roughly chopped
2 tablespoons finely chopped, fresh, flat-leaf parsley
130ml olive oil
Sea salt and freshly ground black pepper

1 Preheat your oven to 180°C/350°F/Gas 4.
2 With a paring knife, trim the stem ends of the okra without opening the pods. Put the vinegar into a large bowl and add the okra. Toss the okra in vinegar and allow to stand for at least 30 minutes and up to a maximum of 1 hour. Drain and rinse under cold water and then spread out in one layer in a large roasting tray.
3 Spread the shallots, peppers and tomatoes over the okra and sprinkle with the chopped parsley.
4 Drizzle the olive oil over the vegetables, season and add 100ml water.
5 Bake in the oven for 40–60 minutes, depending on how well done you like your vegetables. Allow to cool and serve at room temperature.

What goes with what ...
This dish goes well with Cambelo, which is a light red and fruity wine. It is produced by Skouras at Argos in the Peloponnese.

κοτοπουλο στην κατσαρολα με σαλτσα απο καρυδια

chicken thighs braised in walnut sauce

The best walnuts in Greece come from Arcadia in the Peloponnese, and this is a local dish that teams the rich, oily walnuts with the pleasant spiciness of the nutmeg.

8 chicken thighs, skin on
50g butter
2 tablespoons olive oil
2 red onions, peeled and finely chopped
2 bay leaves
1 dessertspoon fresh thyme leaves
200ml milk
2 egg yolks
1 teaspoon grated nutmeg
150g walnuts, crushed in a mortar
Sea salt and freshly ground back pepper

1 Season the chicken thighs with salt and pepper.

2 Take a heavy-bottomed pan and heat the butter and the oil together. When hot but not smoking, add the chopped onions and sauté for 3 or 4 minutes until golden. Reserve in a bowl.

3 Add the chicken thighs to the pan and cook until they too have taken on a golden brown colour. Return the onions to the pan and add the bay leaves and the thyme leaves. Add enough hot water to barely cover the chicken.

4 Cover the pan and leave to simmer for 30–40 minutes, or until the chicken is cooked.

5 Remove the chicken with a straining spoon and keep warm.

6 Strain the cooking liquid into a smaller saucepan and bring to the boil, then reduce it until you have about 800ml.

7 Whisk the milk and egg yolks together in a bowl. Turn down the heat under the sauce and pour the egg mixture into the sauce. Stir continuously until the sauce has thickened and be careful not to let it boil. Add the nutmeg and finally the crushed walnuts. Adjust the seasoning.

8 Leave to simmer for 2–3 minutes to allow the flavours to combine and then pour the sauce over the chicken and serve.

What goes with what ...
This dish goes well with the Minoiko from Crete – a rich white wine that is pleasantly full bodied.

roast partridge
with walnut stuffing

This is a dish for my father. It's a rich dish that will gladden the heart of any dedicated gourmet. Partridges are found throughout the very North of Greece, while the walnut trees are more widely spread. Together these flavours work very well indeed.

4 partridges

zest and juice of 1 lemon

4 rashers of streaky bacon

1 tablespoon butter

100ml red wine

100ml beef or chicken stock (if to hand, otherwise use water)

STUFFING

2 large Spanish onions, peeled and finely chopped

300g leeks, finely sliced

6 cloves of garlic, peeled and crushed

1 tablespoon coriander seeds, roughly ground

100ml olive oil

1 heaped tablespoon chopped fresh coriander

2 tablespoons of celery leaves, chopped

125g crushed walnuts

Sea salt and freshly ground black pepper

1 Preheat the oven – it needs to be very hot - to 230°C/450°F/Gas 8.

2 Rub the partridges with the lemon juice on the inside and out, and then on the inside with the lemon zest. Place to one side.

3 Put the onions, leeks, garlic and ground coriander seeds in a frying pan with the oil and sweat with a lid on, stirring occasionally, until everything is very soft, about 30–40 minutes.

Remove from the heat and add the fresh coriander and celery leaves and crushed walnuts, then adjust the seasoning. Leave until the stuffing is cool enough to handle.

4 Stuff the birds and cover their breasts with the streaky bacon. Truss them (to hold them in shape and secure the bacon) using butcher's string.

5 Place a heavy-bottomed roasting tray on the stove and melt the butter in it. When it is sizzling, start browning the birds. (They need to be well-sealed.)

6 Discard the excess fat and arrange the birds in the tray. Cook in the oven for 10 minutes, then lower the temperature to 200°C/400°F/Gas 6 and leave them for another 15 minutes.

7 Remove the partridges from the tray and leave them somewhere warm to rest for 10 minutes. Put the oven tray over a high heat and deglaze it first with the red wine and then with the stock or water. Bring to the boil and reduce until the sauce has a good consistency.

8 Serve the birds with sauce separately.

What goes with what ...
This dish goes very well with the Trahanas (page 175) and will need a serious red wine with plenty of back-bone – either the Ampellochora from Antonopoulos, or the Cava from Hatzmichalis would do very well.

veal in filo roll

This is a dish that would have originally been made from kid meat, and which comes from Epirus. If you want to make it, you should be left alone in the kitchen as it needs concentration and space.

50g butter

50ml olive oil

2 red onions, peeled and finely chopped

350g pie veal, minced finely

200g plum tomatoes, skinned, deseeded and chopped (or use shop-bought passata)

1 tablespoon ground cinnamon

2 heaped tablespoons fresh basil, chopped

2 medium egg whites

12 sheets of filo pastry

50g butter, melted

2 tablespoons finely chopped fresh, flat-leaf parsley

Sea salt and freshly ground black pepper

BECHAMEL SAUCE

300ml milk

50g butter

50g plain flour

100g grated Kefalotiri cheese (or substitute Pecorino cheese)

2 nutmegs, grated

2 medium egg yolks

1 Heat the butter and the olive oil in a large frying pan. Fry the onions gently until soft, then add the meat and cook until it firms up and stops looking raw.

2 Add the tomatoes and the cinnamon. Cover and simmer gently for 20 minutes, stirring occasionally.

3 Stir in the basil, season to taste and allow to cool down completely. Then whisk the egg whites slightly in a bowl and stir them into the meat with a wooden spoon.

4 Preheat your oven to 180°C/350°F/Gas 4.

5 Make the Béchamel sauce. First, set the milk to heat in a saucepan. Then melt the butter in a frying pan. Stir in the flour and cook the paste gently without letting it colour.

6 Add the hot milk a little at a time, stirring it in well so that each batch is completely absorbed before you add more milk. Then add the grated cheese and the nutmeg; the mixture should now be almost solid.

7 Allow the sauce to cool to room temperature and beat in the egg yolks. Put half the mixture to one side.

8 Now assemble the roll. Layer the sheets of filo by brushing each one with melted butter before placing the next one on top. (Keeping the filo under a damp tea towel will help reduce tearing.) You will end up with a rectangle of buttery pastry.

9 When adding each layer of filling, you must leave a good 3cm margin on all four sides. First, there is the filo and then there should be a rectangle of béchamel with a 3cm margin of bare filo. Then on top of the béchamel there should be a rectangle of minced meat mixture with a 3cm margin of béchamel. On top of the minced meat there should be another rectangle of béchamel with a 3cm margin of meat. Finally, put a strip of chopped parsley down the middle.

10 Now fold in the long edges of the pastry to contain the layers and roll up the parcel. Brush the outside with melted butter. Wrap the sausage of filo and meat loosely in baking parchment, tie with string and place it (pastry seam side down) in a roasting tray.

11 Bake for about 1 hour, but after 50 minutes cut the paper covering with scissors and peel back to allow the top to brown.

What goes with what ...
Serve warm, rather than hot and carve the roll straight across and serve with a crunchy salad. Try it with a glass of Domaine Mercouri, a famously smooth red wine.

> *"Whatever anyone bakes in the oven with onions, tomatoes and breadcrumbs, they end up calling it Spetsai-style"*

fish spetsai-style

There are four islands close to Athens which are known collectively as the Saronic islands. Spetsai is the furthest from Athens and the closest to the Peloponnese, and this classic combination of onions, tomatoes and breadcrumbs is a style that is associated with this particular island.

SERVES 6

25g butter

6 fillets of fish, about 1kg in total (ask your fishmonger for fillets from larger fish that are over 2kg. Choose fine, white fish such as turbot, brill, John Dory, sea bass or red mullet)

Juice of 1 lemon

150ml olive oil

200g shallots, peeled and finely sliced

1 bunch of spring onions, finely chopped

500g tinned plum tomatoes in their juice

100ml white wine

1 tablespoon finely chopped fresh dill

1 tablespoon finely chopped fresh flat-leaf parsley

1 tablespoon finely chopped fresh chervil

40g dry breadcrumbs

Sea salt and freshly ground black pepper

1 Use the butter to grease a roasting tray. Remove any pinbones from the fish fillets and lay them out in the tray. Sprinkle with half the lemon juice and season well. Cover and set aside at room temperature while you begin to prepare the sauce.

2 Preheat your oven to 200°C/400°F/Gas 6.

3 Heat the olive oil in a frying pan and sauté the shallots until they are soft, but not browned. Add the spring onions, tomatoes, wine, dill, parsley and chervil. Leave to simmer until the sauce has thickened.

4 Spread half the tomato sauce over the fish fillets and sprinkle with half the breadcrumbs. Bake in the oven for 6 minutes, then remove the tray and increase the heat to 220°C/425°F/Gas 7.

5 Spread the remaining sauce over the fillets and sprinkle them with the rest of the lemon juice and breadcrumbs. Return the tray to the oven and bake for a further 7 minutes.

What goes with what ...
This classic dish goes well with the Amethystos white, which is made from the Sauvignon Blanc, Asyrtiko and the Semillion grapes.

χοιρινο στο φουρνο με
κυδωνια και φοικασε

pork and quince casserole

An autumnal dish that is an Athenian favourite, this is a splendid combination of flavours. The richness of the pork is teamed with the sharpness of the quinces. If you are unable to get hold of quinces, do not despair: simply chop up two sharp cooking apples roughly and put them inside the pork joint as you roll it up. (You should choose a cooking apple that doesn't turn to mush, so avoid Bramley's.) Because the apples cook much more quickly than the quince they need extra protection, which is why they must go inside.

2 unwaxed lemons

Half a hand of pork (also known as the shoulder), weighing about 1.5kg (get your butcher to bone it out and it will end up weighing just under 1kg)

300ml water

75g unsalted butter

1kg quinces

50ml olive oil

2 whole nutmegs, grated (this is about 1 dessertspoon powdered nutmeg)

2 tablespoons honey

2 tablespoons sugar

Sea salt and freshly ground black pepper

1 Grate the lemon skins and save the zest, then squeeze them and save the juice.

2 Season the pork joint with salt and pepper and rub all over the inside with the lemon zest. Tie it into a roll with butcher's string. Weigh it and make a note of the cooking time: allow 20 minutes per 500g for the cooking time in the oven, in addition to the 30 minutes on top of the stove. Place the joint in a hot frying pan and sear it thoroughly until the outside has a good colour. This is a smoky procedure! Turn on your oven and preheat it to 200°C/400°F/Gas 6.

3 Transfer the pork to a non-reactive metal casserole that is a fairly close fit. Add the water, lemon juice and the butter. Put the lid on and leave to simmer on top of the stove for 30 minutes.

4 Peel the quinces and quarter them. Heat the olive oil in a frying pan and then seal the quinces but be careful not to let them colour. Put them into a bowl and mix thoroughly with the grated nutmeg, honey and sugar. (If you are using apples, stir the nutmeg, honey and sugar into the braising liquid.)

5 Spoon the quince mixture over the top of the pork joint and add a little more water if you think it needs it. Put the lid on and bake in the oven for the cooking time you have worked out earlier.

What goes with what ...
This dish keeps well in a low oven and a long rest prior to serving may actually improve it. Serve it with some crisp roast potatoes, which will add a pleasant contrasting texture. And to drink? Perhaps one of the more full-bodied white wines like the Château Julia Chardonnay, or reds like the Domaine Mercouri from the Mercouri Estate.

minced lamb, kebab-style

This is a recipe that is full of Middle Eastern influences and it comes from the souvlaki place closest to my parents' house in Athens.

SERVES 6

1kg minced shoulder of lamb (ask your butcher to put it through twice)

50g white bread (crusts removed), soaked in milk and squeezed dry

2 cloves of garlic, peeled and crushed

1 large Spanish onion, peeled and finely chopped

1 dessertspoon ground coriander

1 dessertspoon ground allspice

Vegetable oil for frying

6 slices of streaky bacon

6 Middle Eastern flatbreads (you could get away with pitta)

Sea salt and freshly ground black pepper

TOMATO SALAD

620g plum tomatoes

40g fleshy red chilli peppers, deseeded

4 teaspoons red wine vinegar

4 tablespoons extra virgin olive oil

1 teaspoon chopped fresh thyme

Sea salt and freshly ground black pepper

1 Take a large mixing bowl and in it, knead together the lamb mince, bread, garlic, onion, spices and salt and pepper. Cover and put to rest for 1 hour in the fridge.

2 Make up a small "test" patty of the mixture and fry it to check the seasoning (it should taste of the spices). Adjust the salt and pepper as necessary, according to taste.

3 Divide the mixture into 24 equal-sized balls (about 50g each). Knead and flatten them until you have discs of about 1cm thick. Cut the bacon rashers into pieces about 1cm long.

4 Take six thin skewers and put four of the discs onto each one, spacing them out with an upright square of bacon. Wet your hands and use them to shape each finished kebab into a uniform cylinder about 10cm long and about 2cm thick. Roll the skewer like a rolling pin to even things out. Place the skewers on a tray, cover and refrigerate.

5 Make the tomato salad while the kebabs firm up. Chop the tomatoes and chillies roughly and dress with red wine vinegar, extra virgin olive oil, fresh thyme and salt and pepper.

6 Grill the kebabs under a moderate heat, turning every 5 minutes. The bacon should baste the meat. In about 25 minutes the surface should be splendidly crusted and the inside will be cooked, unless you like your meat underdone.

7 Warm the breads and make pockets filled with the tomato salad and a kebab.

What goes with what ...
Tzatziki (page 34) makes a good additional dressing for these kebabs. And rather like kebabs in Britain, beer makes a grand accompaniment to these delicious meat skewers.

cuttlefish with raisins and pine kernels

In this recipe it is traditional to use the ink of the cuttlefish, but as the majority of the cuttlefish in the UK are net-caught, it is hard to come by: the cuttlefish expel their ink when they try to escape. If you are lucky enough to have the ink sacs, crush them in a sieve over a bowl and with the back of a spoon, extract as much ink as possible. (Sometimes far-sighted fishmongers sell small plastic sachets of cuttlefish ink, which work well.) If you have any ink, add it at the same time as the red wine.

SERVES 6

400g leeks, trimmed, washed and
   finely chopped
90ml olive oil
1.5kg cuttlefish (ask your
   fishmonger to clean and cut
   it up)
200ml red wine
350g plum tomatoes, skinned,
   deseeded and coarsely chopped
3 garlic cloves, peeled and finely
   chopped
1kg large leaf spinach, washed
   and left whole
100g raisins
100g pine kernels
4 tablespoons extra virgin olive oil
2 tablespoons fresh flat-leaf
   parsley, finely chopped
3 tablespoons fresh dill, finely
   chopped
Sea salt and freshly ground black
   pepper

1 Take a deep frying pan and sauté the leeks in the olive oil for 4 minutes or until they begin to turn transparent.

2 Add the cuttlefish and continue sautéeing for 8–10 minutes.

3 Flame the frying pan with the red wine and add the chopped tomatoes and garlic. Season with salt and pepper and leave to simmer for 30 minutes.

4 Stir in the washed spinach, raisins and pine kernels, and cook for a further 10 minutes.

5 Dress the dish with the extra virgin olive oil and the fresh herbs.

What goes with what ...
This dish goes very well with tagliatelle or plain rice, and suits the red Notios, which is from the Gaia estate, located in the Peloponnese.

crab claws
stewed with muscat wine

κ α β ο υ ρ α ς   γ ι α χ ν ι

This is a simple, but luxurious dish which is traditionally served with a pilaff made from a soft, white Greek cabbage called Lahano. They are perfect partners – see the recipe on page 171.

150ml olive oil

3 bunches of spring onions, finely chopped (including the green tops)

2 cloves of garlic, peeled and well crushed or pounded in a mortar

400g plum tomatoes, peeled, deseeded and chopped

50ml sweet, white Muscat wine

12 large, raw crab claws, each cracked at a couple of points

4 heaped tablespoons finely chopped fresh dill

Sea salt and freshly ground black pepper

1 Preheat your oven to 180°C/350°F/Gas 4.

2 Place 100ml of the olive oil in a large frying pan, add half the spring onions and fry until they are golden.

3 Add the garlic and stir well. Add the chopped tomatoes and the Muscat wine. Stir and adjust the seasoning with salt and pepper. Cover and simmer for 10–15 minutes to allow the flavours to amalgamate.

4 Check the seasoning again and transfer the sauce to a flat oven dish. Add the crab claws and remaining spring onions, stir well and bake in the oven for 10 minutes.

5 Boil a kettle and then check the dish and re-mix the crab claws in the sauce. (You have to be sure that the sauce has every opportunity to work its way into the cracks in the shell.) If the sauce is becoming dried out at this point, add a little boiling water.

6 Allow to cook for another 10 minutes and then remove from the oven and sprinkle with the chopped dill. Leave to cool as this dish should be served warm, rather than hot.

What goes with what ...
Team the crab claws and Lahano Pilaff with Ilioni, a white wine from Epirus whose sweetness will complement the echoes of Muscat wine in the sauce.

baked eels with feta

This is a regional speciality from the North West of Greece. There are three lakes fringing the Albanian border which are called Prespes. This area is renowned for eel dishes and the local method for skinning the eels involves covering your hands with rock salt to grip the slippery skin. It is much more difficult than it looks! If freshwater eels are not available, you can use conger eel but it won't be as rich and tasty.

1kg eels (ask your fishmonger to skin them and cut them into 4cm lengths)
100ml extra virgin olive oil
1 tablespoon fresh thyme leaves
Zest and juice of 1 lemon
1 tablespoon honey
500ml Tomato Sauce (page 174)
400g good Greek feta, cut into 1cm dice)
2 tablespoons finely chopped fresh mint
Sea salt and freshly ground black pepper

1 Marinate the eel pieces with the olive oil, thyme, half the lemon juice, the grated lemon zest and honey for about 2 hours. Mix the ingredients together and cover in cling film and refrigerate.
2 Preheat your oven to 200°C/400°F/Gas 6.
3 Pour the tomato sauce into a saucepan and keep it warm.
4 Sear the pieces of eel on a dry griddle or frying pan and transfer them to a casserole dish.
5 Pour over the warm tomato sauce and sprinkle the feta over the top.
6 Bake in the oven, uncovered, for 20–30 minutes, by which time the sauce will have started to thicken, the feta will be melting and the eel pieces will be very tender.
7 Check the seasoning: it may need more coarsely ground black pepper and the rest of the lemon juice. Finally, sprinkle the dish with the chopped mint.

What goes with what ...
Serve the eels with something plain to counterbalance the richness. Plain boiled potatoes would be a firm local favourite. Drink Robola – quite a "salty" white wine, which will reflect the saltiness of the feta.

macaroni with mushrooms, unsmoked bacon and cheese

Although from the East of the country, this recipe is very well known all over Greece. A hearty dish that touches all the bases, it is reminiscent of a more superior lasagne and is certainly a cousin to Pastitsio, but it also incorporates a cheese sauce that is a kind of savoury custard.

MUSHROOM AND BACON SAUCE
4 tablespoons olive oil
50g butter
100g leeks, trimmed and finely sliced
1kg wild mushrooms, cleaned (or substitute 1kg Portabello or flat mushrooms, sliced)

1 To make the mushroom and bacon sauce, heat the oil and butter in a frying pan and cook the leeks gently until soft. Add the wild mushrooms and cook on until begin to soften. Remove the leeks and mushrooms and transfer to a bowl. Fry the bacon for 2 or 3 minutes and then transfer to the bowl.
2 Add the red wine to the pan and scrape up any bits that stick to the pan. Pour the juices into the mushroom mixture. Sprinkle over grated nutmeg and mix well. Adjust the seasoning and then mix in the grated cheese. Leave to one side.

250g thinly sliced, unsmoked bacon, rinds removed and cut into strips

100ml red wine

1 nutmeg, grated

100g grated Kefalotiri cheese (or use Pecorino, or even Parmesan cheese)

Sea salt and freshly ground black pepper

MACARONI

1 dessertspoon salt

1 teaspoon olive oil

500g Greek macaroni (If you substitute Italian, you want the long macaroni with a hole down the middle, about the size of a milkshake straw)

50g butter

Freshly ground black pepper

2 medium eggs, beaten

CHEESE SAUCE

4 tablespoons unsalted butter

4 tablespoons plain flour

1 litre whole milk (hot, but not boiling)

100g grated Kefalotiri cheese (or use Pecorino, or even Parmesan cheese)

100g good Greek feta, grated

1 whole nutmeg, grated

6 medium eggs (3 whole and 3 yolks only)

Sea salt and freshly ground black pepper

FOR THE FINAL ASSEMBLY

150g grated Kefalotiri cheese (or use Pecorino, or even Parmesan cheese)

3 Preheat your oven to 180°C/350°F/Gas 4.

4 To cook the macaroni, fill a large pan with plenty of water. Add the salt and the olive oil and bring to the boil. Put the pasta into the pot and cook for 8–10 minutes. (It should be on the firm side of al dente.) Leave the macaroni to strain through a colander while you add the butter to the hot pan. Add the macaroni, stir well and add several twists of freshly ground black pepper.

5 Transfer the pasta to a large bowl and stir in the beaten eggs. Set aside.

6 To make the cheese sauce, melt the butter in a saucepan and add the flour, stirring as it cooks to a pale beige coloured paste. Gradually work in the hot milk, a little at a time, stirring constantly until you have a smooth sauce. Add the grated cheese, nutmeg and seasoning. Cook for 4 minutes or until all is smooth, check the seasoning and adjust. Set aside to cool for 10 minutes.

7 Whisk the eggs and egg yolks together in a bowl and then whisk them into the cool sauce.

8 To assemble, take a large oven dish (about 30 x 20 x 7cm). Layer the ingredients - macaroni, mushroom sauce, cheese sauce; repeat – macaroni, mushroom, cheese sauce and finally, sprinkle with the extra grated cheese.

9 Bake in the oven and after 40 minutes, test the dish. If a knife inserted into the middle comes out clean, it is done. Do not cut it immediately; let it rest for 1 hour to set before serving.

What goes with what ...

Greek housewives and lazy restaurateurs are particularly fond of this dish as it is best eaten when it is lukewarm and will therefore keep improving, however late the guests become. It needs a nice, honest red wine like the Nemea from Boutari.

γαριδες σαγανακι
με φετα

crevettes with feta and tomato sauce

As soon as the first warm sunshine comes after the winter and the seaside restaurants start to put tables outside, this is their star dish. It seems as though the whole of Athens makes the journey to Sounio to eat prawns. As with most prawn dishes, you should start with the largest, freshest prawns you can buy. Fresh prawns are glossy, they smell of the sea without a hint of ammonia and do not need rinsing.

750ml Tomato Sauce (page 174)
250g Greek feta cheese, crumbled
50ml olive oil
1 bunch of spring onions, finely chopped
3 cloves of garlic, peeled and crushed
2 tablespoons fresh thyme leaves
16 Mediterranean crevettes weighing about 40g or 16 Tiger prawns
70ml Ouzo
30ml extra virgin olive oil
Freshly ground black pepper

1 Preheat your oven to 180°C/350°F/Gas 4. Take a large, flat oven dish and pour the tomato sauce into it. Scatter the feta over the top and put it into the oven for 5 minutes until the feta is melting.

2 Take a large frying pan and heat 25ml of the ordinary olive oil in it. Add the spring onions, garlic and thyme. Sweat for 5 minutes or until the onions are soft, then stir them into the tomato sauce in the oven dish. Return the dish to the oven to keep warm.

3 Put the frying pan back on the heat, add the remaining ordinary olive oil and sear the crevettes for 2 or 3 minutes. Then flame the pan with the Ouzo. When the flames have died down, add the crevettes and the pan juices to the oven dish full of tomato sauce. Season with black pepper and mix everything together and return to the oven for a further 10 minutes to allow the flavours to amalgamate.

4 Remove the dish from the oven and pour the extra virgin olive oil over the top. Allow to cool a little before serving.

What goes with what ...
This dish should be allowed to cool a little so that it can be eaten messily, by hand, with some good bread. It goes well with a wine that is bone dry, but not too highly acidic, such as the Thalassitis which is made by Gaia.

σουβλακια απο μπακαλιαρο και καπαρι με αμπελοφυλλα

salted cod kebabs

This is one of the typical dishes of the border towns between Turkey and Greece. Eighty per cent of the salt cod in Greece originates from the Black Sea and it tends to be a little more salty than its British counterpart.

1kg home-salted cod, cured for
   3 days (page 178)

5 medium slices of bread, without
   the crusts

75ml extra virgin olive oil

Zest of 1 lemon

4 tablespoons finely chopped dill
   weed

200g capers, soaked and rinsed to
   remove the salt

Freshly ground black pepper

16 blanched vine leaves

About 16 kebab sticks

4 tablespoons finely chopped
   flat-leaf parsley

FOR BASTING

1 tablespoon Dijon mustard

Juice of 2 lemons

50ml olive oil

2 tablespoons finely chopped
   thyme

1 teaspoon freshly ground black
   pepper

1 Rinse the cod fillet well and cut it into strips lengthways (about 2cm) wide and then into pieces of about 4cm long so that you can roll them up.

2 In a mixing bowl mash the bread, extra virgin olive oil, lemon zest, dill and capers together. Season with pepper.

3 Smear the bread mix onto a piece of cod (like a pinwheel). Then wrap it with a vine leaf and secure with a kebab stick. Repeat until all the cod is used up. Set to one side.

4 Make the baste by dissolving the mustard in the lemon juice, then whisk in the olive oil, thyme and black pepper.

5 To cook the kebabs, brush them liberally with the baste and then cook them under a preheated hot grill (or on a barbecue) for 15 minutes, basting regularly and turning as necessary.

What goes with what ...
Sprinkle with fresh parsley and serve with homemade chips, radishes and yoghurt, which are the traditional accompaniments. Drink Tselepos Mantinea, an upfront white wine.

σφυριδα βραστη με υποξινα σταφιλια
poached fish with green grape sauce

This is one of a few recipes which stem from the ancient Greek tradition of using verjuice (the juice from unripe grapes) as a souring agent rather than lemon juice. It's a favourite on the Aegean islands.

SERVES 6

1 x meaty, round and white-fleshed fish weighing about 2kg (use grouper if you can or a firm, white fish such as cod. Ask your fishmonger to prepare as 6 fillets and remove the pin bones. (Retain the bones, trimmings and head)
750g peeled new potatoes
300g carrots, peeled and cut on the diagonal into 2cm chunks
300g leeks (only the white part), left whole
2 tablespoons finely chopped fresh dill
Sea salt and freshly ground black pepper

FISH STOCK
Fish bones, trimmings and head (as above)
50g carrots, roughly chopped
50g leeks, roughly chopped
2 tablespoons roughly chopped fresh flat-leaf parsley
50g fennel, roughly chopped
1 bay leaf
4 litres water

SAUCE
60ml extra virgin olive oil
150g leeks, washed, trimmed and finely chopped
1kg sharp, green seedless grapes
4 tablespoons honey

1. Put all the ingredients for the stock into a large stockpot. Simmer for 1 hour: the stock should taste of fish. Pass it through an extra-fine sieve, wash the pot and put the stock back into it.

2 To make the sauce, heat the olive oil in a deep frying pan and gently sauté the chopped leeks until transparent. Add the grapes and the honey and leave to simmer for a further 15 minutes. Taste and adjust the seasoning. Put to one side and keep warm.

3 Season your fish fillets with salt and pepper and place to one side while you bring the large pot of fish stock to simmering point and then add the vegetables. Cook for about 25 minutes, by which time the vegetables should be soft.

4 Lower the fish fillets into the stock and poach them for 10–12 minutes depending on how thick they are. They are done when they are cooked but still firm.

5 Remove the fish and vegetables with the help of a slotted spoon and place them on a serving platter. Pour over the warm green grape sauce, add the chopped dill and serve.

What goes with what ...
Try this dish with the elegant white wine from Santorini, called Thalassitis.

poached rack of lamb with fennel

 αρνάκι με μάραθο

This is an elegant dish and because the lamb is poached in a light broth there is never any suspicion of dry meat. The timings given will produce lamb that is cooked to "the pink side of well done". If you like your meat cooked a little more, it is a simple matter: just leave it in a while longer. Indeed, you can fish out the rack, carve off a chop and if it is not to your liking, put the whole thing back in to cook some more. Insist that your butcher de-fats the lamb rigorously before you take it home.

3 cloves of garlic, peeled and left whole

1 rack of lamb, weighing about 1kg before trimming

2 lemons

1kg fennel, leaves picked and finely chopped (save any feathery tops)

100ml extra virgin olive oil

2 litres homemade chicken stock (or jellied stock from the supermarket; dilute with water so that it is half the recommended strength)

250g shallots, peeled and left whole

130g peeled new potatoes, left whole

100g carrots, peeled and chopped

100g leeks, finely chopped (including the green parts)

2 stalks of celery, finely chopped

4 bay leaves

1 heaped tablespoon finely chopped flat-leaf parsley

1 heaped tablespoon finely chopped dill weed

Sea salt and freshly ground black pepper

1 Take the garlic cloves and cut them into slivers. Use a sharp knife to insert them into the meaty part of the lamb.

2 Grate the zest from the lemons and mix it in a bowl with the fennel, 1 tablespoon of sea salt and 1 tablespoon of freshly ground black pepper, and half the extra virgin olive oil.

3 Rub the mixture into the rack of lamb, wrap in cling film and leave in the fridge to marinate overnight.

4 Take a non-reactive saucepan, large enough to hold the rack of lamb and the vegetables, pour in the stock and bring it to the boil. Add the vegetables and the bay leaves and leave to simmer until the fennel is cooked, about 45 minutes to 1 hour, skimming occasionally, if necessary.

5 After the first 45 minutes chop the parsley and the dill (reserve a little of both for presentation) and add the remaining olive oil. Check the amount of liquid in the pot: there must be enough to immerse the rack of lamb. If needs be, add some boiling water. Season to taste with sea salt and pepper.

6 Submerge the rack of lamb in the simmering soup and cook for 15 minutes. Lift it out and carve into cutlets. Add the juice of one of the lemons to the broth and check the seasoning one last time.

7 Serve the broth in bowls with the cutlets arranged around the edge. Sprinkle with the last of the dill and parsley.

What goes with what ...
The delicacy of the lamb, and the faint flavour of aniseed which comes from the fennel, would go well with one of the new-style fruity red wines, such as the Skouras Megas Oenos – a mixture of Cabernet Sauvignon and Agiorgitiko from the Peloponnese.

ismir meatballs in tomato sauce

When the Real Greek restaurant opened, this was one of the runaway successes, despite a heated debate between all concerned as to just what it should be called in English. Were they meatballs, dumplings, or even rissoles? Whatever their name, they are certainly delicious. Armed with this recipe, meatballs should never be boring again.

500g minced lamb (ask your butcher for neck fillet and to run it twice through the mincer)

250g white bread, crusts removed (soak the bread in milk and squeeze the slices until almost dry)

1 tablespoon powdered cumin

1 small onion, peeled and finely chopped

4 cloves of garlic, peeled and crushed

50g pitted and cracked green olives, roughly chopped

1 medium egg, beaten

Boiled, white long-grain rice to serve

50g plain flour

olive oil for frying

150ml pot Greek yoghurt

1 dessertspoon cumin seeds

Sea salt and freshly ground black pepper

Sea salt and freshly ground black pepper

SAUCE

1 x 560g jar tomato passata

100ml extra virgin olive oil

1 teaspoon sugar

1 x 400g tin plum tomatoes

1 parcel of muslin-wrapped spices (2 cinnamon sticks, 3 cloves, 2 bay leaves and 1 dessertspoon cumin seeds)

150g small white pickling onions, peeled

50g pitted and cracked green olives

1 Start by making the meatballs so that you can rest them while you make the sauce. Knead the minced lamb with the breadcrumbs, powdered cumin, chopped onion, garlic, olives and the beaten egg. Season the mixture with salt and freshly ground black pepper.

2 Wet your hands and mould the mix into spheres, about 2cm in diameter. Leave them in the fridge to allow the flavours to amalgamate.

3 To make the sauce, take a large non-reactive saucepan and add the jar of passata, 80ml olive oil and the sugar. Pass the tinned tomatoes and their juice through a sieve into the pan. They will add extra flavour to the ready-made passata. Season with salt and freshly ground black pepper, add the muslin-wrapped spices and leave the sauce to simmer for 30 minutes. Remember to skim regularly.

4 Add the onions to the pan and allow the sauce to simmer for another hour until they are cooked, then cook for a further 20 minutes.

5 Blanch the remaining cracked olives in boiling water for 2 minutes and add them to the tomato sauce. Leave to simmer gently with the lid on.

6 Roll the meatballs in flour and pan fry them in a little olive oil to brown them and firm them up before you cook them in the sauce.

7 Take 150ml Greek yoghurt and stir the cumin seeds into it. Cover and leave to cool in the fridge.

8 Bring the sauce to simmering point, add the meatballs and leave to simmer with the lid on until cooked, about 15 minutes.

What goes with what ...
Serve the Ismir Meatballs on boiled white, long-grain rice, with the sauce in which they were cooked, plus the cool cumin yoghurt on the side. The acidity of the tomato sauce could make this a difficult dish to pair with wine, but the well-balanced flavours save the day – choose a rich red wine like Notios.

fish stifado

Stifado is something of a general term and refers to any casserole with lots of white baby onions, vinegar and spicy seasonings. This fish stifado is a pretty "élite" affair and would sit uneasily if called fish stew!

125ml extra virgin olive oil

3 bay leaves

3 cloves

2 cloves of garlic, peeled and crushed

1 kg baby white onions (or small shallots), peeled

100ml red wine

500g plum tomatoes, skinned and deseeded, then puréed (or a jar of supermarket passata)

1 x 1kg raw lobster

500g John Dory, filleted

500g monkfish, filleted

1 heaped tablespoon finely chopped parsley

4 heaped tablespoons finely chopped fennel leaves

50ml white wine vinegar

Sea salt and freshly ground black pepper

1 Place 80ml olive oil in a large saucepan and heat it until the oil is hot, but not smoking. Add the bay leaves, cloves and a few twists of black pepper. Let them sizzle for 2–3 minutes.

2 Add the crushed garlic and the baby white onions, and season with salt. Give them a stir, put the lid on and cook gently for 20 minutes.

3 Add the red wine and tomato juice. Cook, uncovered, for a further 20 minutes, then adjust the seasoning.

4 Slice the lobster lengthways, remove the claws and crack them. Place it all on top of the onion mixture, replace the lid and cook for 5 minutes.

5 Add the fish fillets and cook for another 5-8 minutes. Remove from the heat and add the chopped herbs, the remaining olive oil and the vinegar.

What goes with what ...
This dish goes well with the Adolis Ghis made by Antonopoulos and the Moschophilero from Boutari.

"You've made a real salad of that fish"

(when the cook has made a mess of something)

minced meat purses

A dish that comes from Macedonia. These are small purses made from ravioli dough gathered together around a savoury veal mince, which is flavoured with mint.

MAKES 12 PURSES

500 g strong white flour
1 medium egg
3 teaspoons salt
6 teaspoons extra virgin olive oil
100ml water
125g butter
1 litre chicken stock
Cayenne pepper for dusting

FILLING

500g veal mince
1 medium onion, puréed in a food
    processor
2 dessertspoons of finely chopped
    fresh mint
1 medium egg, beaten
Sea salt and freshly ground black
    pepper

SAUCE

400g Greek yoghurt
3 spring onions, trimmed and
    finely chopped (including most
    of the green part)
3 cloves of garlic, peeled and
    puréed

1 Preheat your oven to 180°C/350°F/Gas 4.

2 To make the dough, put the flour onto a flat surface and make a well in the centre. In a bowl, whisk the egg with the salt and olive oil, then add to the well. Bring the flour into the egg and mix together. Add the water a little at a time, until you have an even dough. As flour is so variable, the 100ml water measure should be taken as a guide. Work the dough until it is elastic. Wrap it in cling film and put it into the fridge to rest for 20 minutes.

3 To make the filling, knead the minced veal in a bowl with the onion purée, mint and the beaten egg. Season.

4 Roll out the dough until it is 5mm thick. Cut it into squares of 5 x 5cm.

5 Place a small spoonful of filling on each square and draw up the corners to form a purse shape. Pinch each one shut carefully. (Use a pastry brush and a little water to "glue" the edges if you have to.)

6 Use a third of the butter to grease a metal roasting tray. Stand the purses upright in the tray and pack them together closely. Add a splash of boiling water and cook the purses over a low heat until they have taken on a little colour, about 5 minutes.

7 Pour the stock over the purses and dot with another third of butter. Cook in the oven for about 20 minutes. Check regularly after 10 minutes and if all the liquid has been absorbed before the purses are cooked, add a little hot water.

8 To prepare the sauce, combine the yoghurt, spring onions and puréed garlic in a bowl and mix thoroughly. Melt the remaining butter in a pan. To assemble, pour the yoghurt mix over the purses and then the melted butter. Finally, dust with cayenne pepper.

What goes with what ...
In Macedonia these are often served on top of a bed of cooked chickpeas. Accompany them with a meaty red wine like the Domaine Mercouri.

roast chicken with yoghurt

This is a Cretan favourite and on the face of it, it looks like a rather strange way of going about things. Persevere: it is certainly worthwhile, just do not expéct it to be a dish with a well behaved sauce in the French idiom.

2 unwaxed lemons
1 x 1.5kg chicken
75ml extra virgin olive oil
150g butter
175ml water
500ml Greek yoghurt
3 medium eggs
Sea salt and freshly ground black
    pepper

1 Grate the lemon skins and save the zest, then squeeze them and save the juice.

2 Wash the outside of the chicken with the lemon juice and rub the zest into the cavity. Cover the chicken and put it into the fridge to marinate for about 2–3 hours.

3 Preheat your oven to 220°C/425°F/Gas 7. Remove the marinade and place the chicken on a roasting tray. Season it well and pour over the oil, butter and 100ml water. Roast it for 20 minutes.

4 Turn the oven down to 180°C/350°F/Gas 4 and continue to roast for a further 50 minutes.

5 Put the yoghurt, eggs and the remaining 75ml of water into a mixing bowl and beat together. Pour the mixture over the chicken and return to the oven for 15 minutes, or until the yoghurt has thickened.

What goes with what ...
The pan scrapings make a delicious sauce for the chicken, which may be served with a rice pilaff. For an accompanying drink, a rich red like Amethystos would be perfect, or the Château Julia Chardonnay.

beef in broth

Every nation has a traditional long-cooked, boiled meat dish in its repertoire. The French have Pot au Feu, the Americans are proud of pot roasts and this is the rich Greek equivalent.

SERVES 6

1 marrow bone, cut across into three pieces

1 whole shin (about 3kg) of beef on the bone (ask your butcher to bone and roll the joint, and to give you the bone cut in two)

4 bay leaves

4 garlic cloves, peeled and left whole

1kg shallots, peeled and left whole

1kg carrots, peeled and sliced 5mm thick

1kg new potatoes, scrubbed and left whole

Sea salt and freshly ground black pepper

1 Take your largest stockpot – 10 litres is not too big – and add the marrow bone and the shin bone to it. Fill with water, place over the heat and bring to the boil. Reduce the heat and simmer for 2 hours, skimming carefully for the first hour. Do not be put off by the scum from the marrow, simply skim it off; it will add flavour and richness to the broth.

2 After 2 hours add the roll of beef shin, the bay leaves and garlic cloves, and some salt and pepper. Put the lid on and continue to cook.

3 After 2$\frac{1}{2}$ hours take the lid off and let the steam out. Add the whole shallots and a bit more seasoning and continue to cook.

4 After another hour, add the carrots and then, after another 30 minutes add the potatoes.

5 When the potatoes are ready (in another 15 minutes), the meat should be on the point of falling apart.

6 To serve, remove the joint of beef and carve into large chunks. Place each chunk in a serving bowl and add the vegetables and consommé.

What goes with what ...

This dish should be accompanied by Mustard Mayonnaise and Ladolemono Sauce (pages 175 and 125). It is also great for "left-over" dishes and for sandwiches when cold. The broth can be reheated with tagliatelle or medium-grain rice. Drink Kava, which in Greek means "aged", a red Hazimichalis from Atlandis, North of Athens.

beef stifado

This dish always took a long time to prepare and was both laborious and fiddly, but by the time it was ready, it was invariably well-received, perhaps due to the amount of wine that was drunk while we were waiting for it. My mother would also have to pre-order extra bread from the local bakery as the gravy is so good.

SERVES 6

60ml olive oil

1.5kg stewing beef (chuck or lean brisket), cut into bite-sized chunks

4 bay leaves

1 ground cinnamon stick, about 3cm long

2 whole nutmegs, grated

1 teaspoon powdered cloves

1 teaspoon ground cumin

3 cloves garlic, peeled and finely chopped

40ml red wine vinegar (aged Greek wine vinegar for preference)

400g plum tomatoes, peeled, deseeded and sieved to give juice

4 tablespoons red wine

1.5kg shallots, peeled but left whole

50g butter

2 tablespoons tomato purée

4 tablespoons finely chopped flat-leaf parsley (including the stalks)

Sea salt and freshly ground black pepper

1 Preheat your oven to 150°C/300°F/Gas 2.

2 Take a heavy-bottomed casserole, heat the olive oil in it and brown the meat to sear the outside edges.

3 As the meat browns, add the bay leaves, cinnamon, nutmeg, cloves, cumin and garlic and let the oil get the flavours from the aromatics.

4 Add the vinegar, let it sizzle for 3–4 minutes and then add the tomato juice and enough hot water to cover the meat. Check the seasoning, add the red wine and arrange the onions on the top of the meat. If you want the shallots to keep their shape, simply score a cross into the base of each one. Add the butter. Give a good shake to the casserole, cover with kitchen foil and then with the lid. Place in an oven for 2^1/$_2$–3 hours. The meat should be very soft at the end of the cooking time.

5 Remove from the oven, stir in the tomato purée and add the chopped parsley to the juices. Stir again and season to taste.

What goes with what ...

Serve immediately with egg noodles and grated Kefalotiri cheese (you could substitute a zingy Pecorino if you cannot get Kefalotiri), or rice. With this dish you should really go for it: try a rich and red wine - Naoussa Grand Reserva, or perhaps Mega Oenos.

baked lobster

* αστακος πλακι*

This dish comes from the island of Astypalea, which has some of the world's finest beaches. It is also the home of excellent saffron and so the lobster is eaten with a saffron pilaff.

2 x 1kg raw lobsters (ask your
    fishmonger to kill them and
    take them straight home to the
    kitchen, or kill them yourself by
    splitting the head in half
    lengthways. DO NOT substitute
    cooked lobster)

125g shallots, peeled and finely
    chopped

125g leeks (the white parts),
    washed and finely chopped

75ml olive oil

3 cloves of garlic, peeled and
    finely chopped

600g good-quality tomato passata

150ml Muscat of Patras or other
    sweet white wine

2 bay leaves

30g finely chopped fennel

2 tablespoons finely chopped
    fresh flat-leaf parsley

125ml extra virgin olive oil

2 tablespoons finely chopped
    fresh mint

Sea salt and freshly ground black
    pepper

1 Split your lobsters in half lengthways. Discard the stomach sacs and keep the livers (these look greenish) and the coral (the eggs) to one side if you are making the traditional Astypalean garnish, which is a kind of "lobster pâté" spread on hot bread. Crack the lobster claws with the back of a knife.

2 Preheat your oven to 200°C/400°F/Gas 6.

3 Take a large frying pan, add the chopped shallots, leeks and olive oil and sauté gently until transparent.

4 Add the garlic and cook for another minute. Then add the passata, sweet white wine and the bay leaves. Stir until mixed together thoroughly. Leave to simmer for 15–20 minutes, stirring occasionally. Add the chopped fennel and parsley and cook for 5 extra minutes. Season to taste.

5 Arrange the halved lobsters in a roasting tray, season and then pour over the hot tomato sauce and 75ml of the extra virgin olive oil. Bake in the oven for 15 minutes.

6 Remove from the oven, sprinkle over the remaining extra virgin olive oil and the chopped mint.

7 Serve hot with warm bread and the liver and coral spread (see below).

What goes with what ...
Try this with the traditional lobster coral and liver spread. Put the lobster's liver and coral into a liquidizer with a little extra virgin oil and liquidize it until you've got a smooth paste. Season and spread over hot bread. Drink sparkling Odi Panos – eating lobster is always a cause for a celebration.

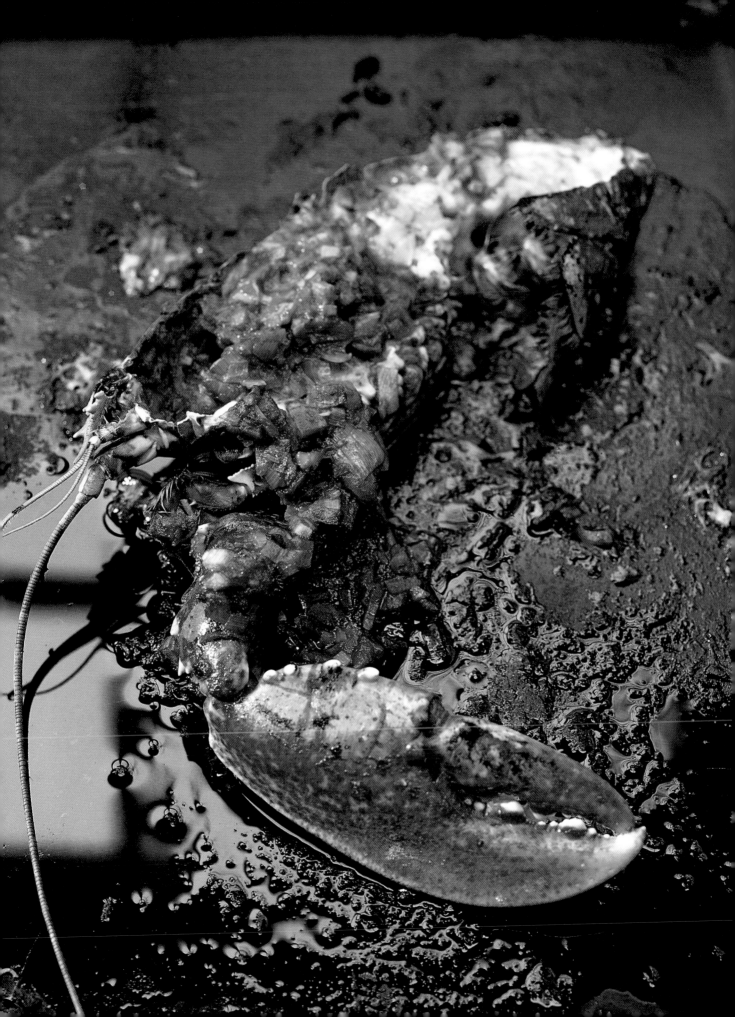

κουκια με γιαουρτι
broad beans with yoghurt

When the first broad beans hit the street markets they coincided with the school reports for the second term. If my results were less than perfect, my penance would be hours spent podding broad beans, during which ordeal I would also have to explain my reports to my mother. It's a wonder that I still like broad beans.

1kg fresh broad beans
100ml extra virgin olive oil
200g shallots, peeled and finely chopped
2 dessertspoons finely chopped flat-leaf parsley
200ml Greek yoghurt
3 dessertspoons finely chopped fresh mint
Sea salt and freshly ground black pepper

1 First, pod the beans. If the beans are very young, you can eat them without removing the inner skins. Otherwise you need to blanch them in salted water for a couple of minutes and then peel them.
2 Heat the oil in a frying pan and sauté the shallots until soft and transparent. Stir in the broad beans, parsley and season. Add hot water from the kettle to barely cover the beans. Put the lid on and simmer until beans are tender.
3 Strain off the cooking liquid into a jug and allow it to cool, then combine 130ml of the cooled cooking liquid with the yoghurt and warm through, stirring all the time.
4 Pour the sauce over the beans and then sprinkle with the chopped mint. Adjust the seasoning if necessary and serve.

What goes with what ...
Eat warm with Cheese Triangles (page 22). It is always hard to partner broad beans with wine, but try the Chateau Julia Chardonnay.

αρνακι στον φουρνο
με ξεροψημενη πετσα
roast lamb ribs with crackling

No self-respecting garden in Athens would be without its own permanent barbecue and this dish ideally needs to be cooked over an open fire out of doors. However, here is a way to make it work indoors.

SERVES 8

1 piece of lamb that combines the "best end" and "breast" (approximate weight 3kg)
Grated zest and juice of 1 lemon
40ml olive oil
2 tablespoons finely chopped fresh thyme
Sea salt and freshly ground black pepper

1 Preheat your oven to 170°C/325°F/Gas 3.
2 Rub the best end and breast of lamb with the lemon juice and olive oil.
3 Mix the salt, pepper, thyme and lemon zest in a mixing bowl. With the back of a wooden spoon, open out a hole from the best end to the other end.
4 Season the best end through the hole and rub the seasoning into the breast.
5 Put the lamb on a roasting tray and place it in the oven for 3–3½ hours. To check if it is ready, either use a meat thermometer (the temperature of the thickest part of the joint should read 80°C/176°F), or wait until the meat between the ribs is falling apart.

What goes with what ...
The crackling is crisp and delicious with bread, a serving of Maroulosalata (page 123) and a glass of Ramnista – a grand, spicy red wine.

pot-roasted aubergines with liver

συκωτάκια με μελιτζάνες

This recipe comes from Kasos, which is in the Dodecanese. It is a classic dish of the Eastern islands, and the interesting and somewhat unexpected background flavour is provided by mint. Be warned: the cooked liver is quite firm, which provides a good counterpoint to the soft aubergine.

2 medium aubergines
90ml extra virgin olive oil
1 x 350g jar of passata
2 bunches of spring onions, trimmed and chopped
200g plum tomatoes, skinned, deseeded and roughly chopped
1 heaped tablespoon finely chopped flat-leaf parsley
6 sprigs of fresh mint
4 tablespoons red wine vinegar
250g lamb's liver
250g pig's liver
Sea salt and freshly ground black pepper

1 Preheat your oven to 180°C/350°F/Gas 4.
2 Slice the aubergines across in rings of 1cm thickness. Salt both sides and let them stand for 30 minutes. Rinse in cold water and drain carefully.
3 Pour the olive oil and passata into a casserole. Mix well and season.
4 Layer the aubergine into the pot with the spring onions, chopped tomatoes, flat-leaved parsley and mint.
5 Sprinkle the vinegar over the top. Cut the liver into small chunks and tuck it in among the aubergine. Cover the pot with foil to seal it and replace the lid.
6 Bake in the oven until the aubergines are soft and the sauce has thickened nicely, about 50–60 minutes.

What goes with what ...
This makes a good one-pot meal. Try it with Ampellochora, an oaky red made from the Agiortiko and Mavrodaphne grapes in the Peloponnese.

lamb with cannellini beans

σουνάκι με φασολάδα

Take the recipe for cannellini beans on page 44 and roast some lamb to go with it. Beans and lamb are one of the world's great combinations and you can pep up the beans with some sliced sausage. The Greek sausage called Soutzoukaki, which is a kind of rich beef sausage, goes particularly well.

A whole "neck" of lamb chops (ask your butcher to prepare 4 pieces, each containing 4 chops and "French" trimmed, that is to say with all the fat removed)
1 clove of garlic, peeled and crushed
1 tablespoon finely chopped fresh flat-leaf parsley
1 tablespoon finely chopped fresh mint
Sea salt and freshly ground black pepper
Cannellini beans, to serve

1 Preheat your oven to 200°C/400°F/Gas 6.
2 Rub the meat with the garlic and herbs and season well.
3 Roast in the oven for 12 minutes (a little longer if you like your lamb well done) and rest for 10 minutes.
4 Slice and serve on top of the cannellini beans.

What goes with what ...
Try this with the red Ramnista from Kyr-Yiannis Boutari, who specializes in these full-bodied wines.

μπακαλιαρο σκορδαλια
fried salt cod
with skordalia

This dish is traditionally eaten in Greece on Twelfth Night (January 6th). It is simple, but contains a stunning combination of flavours.

700g salt cod (page 178)
300ml milk
200g white self raising flour
330ml lager beer
Sea salt
Vegetable oil for frying

1 Soak the salt cod in water overnight, drain thoroughly and then poach it in the milk for about 5 minutes until barely tender. Take it out, leave to cool and remove the skin and any bones. Cut it into four portions.

2 To make the batter, in a bowl mix 200g flour into the lager until you have a smooth batter. Add a pinch of salt.

3 Pour the oil into a frying pan (it should be about 1cm deep) and heat until hot, but not smoking.

4 Sprinkle the remaining 50g flour onto a plate and roll the cod portions in it so that the batter will stick. Dip them in the batter and fry. Cook, turning as necessary, until the batter is a golden tan colour.

What goes with what ...
Serve the cod with Skordalia (page 34). Liven the Skordalia up with about 75ml fish stock. Make this by cooking 40g salt cod in 150ml boiling water. Cook it down until you have the stock you need. This method will take most of the salt from the cod, but should you prefer it a bit more salty, do not poach it for so long, or even omit that stage entirely. It goes well with a glass of Tselepos Mantinea.

octopus stew

It is strange how a dish made from something so very, very fishy can end up tasting so meaty. The secret lies in cooking the octopus until it is very, very tender and all the salty, iodine flavour has filtered into the sauce.

SERVES 8

2kg octopus (frozen octopus works well in this recipe as the freezer tenderizes it. You should always buy the octopus with the double row of suckers)

1 x 4cm stick of cinnamon

2 cloves

1 dessertspoon coriander seeds

1 dessertspoon black peppercorns

3 bay leaves

100ml olive oil

150ml red wine

1kg baby onions, peeled

50ml Greek aged red wine vinegar (or good-quality French red wine vinegar)

4 tablespoons tomato purée

Egg noodles (hilopites) or the tiny Greek nibs of pasta known as Kritharaki and grated Kefalotiri cheese to serve

1 Clean the octopus (or ask your fishmonger). Cut it into small chunks of about 2.5cm.

2 Take a pestle and mortar (or a coffee grinder or food processor – be careful not to overgrind the spices) and roughly grind the cinnamon, cloves, coriander seeds and black peppercorns together. Crumple the bay leaves into the mixture.

3 Pour the olive oil into a heavy-bottomed pot, add the spices and allow the flavours to infuse over a medium heat. Place the octopus pieces in the hot oil and stir well. Put the lid on and leave to simmer for 15–20 minutes, by which time the octopus should be submerged in its own liquid.

4 Add the red wine and the onions. Put the lid back on and allow to cook for a further 45–60 minutes, or until the octopus is very tender and the onions are falling apart.

5 Remove the pot from the heat and add the red wine vinegar and tomato purée. Give the mixture a good stir and let it cool down in the pot.

6 Serve at room temperature, by which time you should have a thick sauce. When you refrigerate the dish, the sauce will set. If you do keep it for a day or two, do not add water; simply reheat very gently and allow the sauce to melt.

What goes with what ...
This stew eats very well with egg noodles (hilopites) or the tiny pasta nibs (kritharaki). When served, it needs a good sprinkling of grated kefalotiri cheese. Drink Cambello with this dish.

rabbit with avgolemono sauce

κουνελι αυγολεμονο

Rabbits are often kept within the home in Athens, especially for cooking. My grandmother would show off her lack of squeamishness when it was time to eat; we children watched in awe.

1 rabbit weighing about 1kg (with the heart, kidneys and liver, if possible)

200ml olive oil

250g shallots, peeled and left whole

100g streaky bacon, rinds removed and cut into strips

100ml white wine

750g rocket (or as a cheaper option, curly endive)

2 Cos lettuces

3 bunches of spring onions, trimmed

SAUCE

2 medium eggs, separated

Juice of 2 lemons

Sea salt and freshly ground black pepper

1 You can either ask your butcher to cut the rabbit into small chunks or do it yourself. Remember to keep the offal.

2 Season the rabbit well. Put half the oil into a heavy-bottomed frying pan and sear the rabbit pieces. Remove and keep warm in a large metal casserole while you sauté the shallots, bacon and rabbit offal in the same frying pan.

3 When the shallots are soft, deglaze the pan with the white wine and add the contents to the rabbit in the casserole. Add just enough water to cover everything and cook over a low heat, with the lid on, for about 10 minutes.

4 Meanwhile, tear the rocket (or endive) and the Cos lettuces into manageable pieces, and roughly chop the spring onions including most of the green parts. Parboil them in boiling, salted water for 5–10 minutes. Drain and add the greens to the rabbit.

5 Keep the heat very low and cook for a further 10–15 minutes until the rabbit is tender.

6 Make the avgolemono sauce. Take two egg whites and whisk in a bowl until they form soft peaks. Then, a little at a time, incorporate the egg yolks and the lemon juice, finally working in a little (about 150ml) of the liquid that the rabbit is cooking in.

7 Finally, take the casserole off the heat and add the egg sauce, plus the remaining olive oil. Stir well and let the casserole rest, off the heat, for 15 minutes before serving.

What goes with what ...
Being quite rich, the Avgolemono sauce poses a problem when choosing a wine, but the Amethystos red has enough body to cope.

casseroled quail
with tomatoes and pilaff

This is a dish from Epirus, where if truth were told, they would be happy to make it from any of the smallest, prettiest songbirds that they could catch, trap or shoot. Quail are bigger, and better eating!

8 oven-ready quail

Juice of 3 lemons

2 heaped tablespoons fresh
   coriander, finely chopped

4 tablespoons olive oil

75g butter

2 red onions, peeled and finely
   chopped

200g plum tomatoes, skinned,
   deseeded and finely chopped
   (or use shop-bought passata)

100g plum tomatoes, peeled and
   liquidized

1 stick of cinnamon, about
   5cm long

500ml chicken stock

250g long-grain rice

Sea salt and freshly ground black
   pepper

1 Preheat your oven to 190°C/375°F/Gas 5.

2 Rub the quail with the lemon juice, then rub them with finely chopped coriander and season with salt and pepper. Put to one side.

3 Take a heavy-bottomed metal casserole and add to it the olive oil and 35g butter. Sauté the onions until soft, but not coloured. Add the chopped tomatoes and season.

4 Arrange the quail in the casserole and pour the tomato juice over them. Add the cinnamon stick (break it in half). The quail should be barely covered, so top up the casserole with hot water from the kettle. Bake in the oven for 25–35 minutes.

5 Remove the casserole from the oven and strain off the liquid into a measuring jug. Throw away the solid bits. Take out the quail and keep them somewhere warm. Make the liquid up to 600ml with hot chicken stock. Add the rice, stir well and season to taste.

6 Cook the rice, uncovered on the top of the stove, for 15 minutes or until the rice has absorbed all the liquid. Add more hot water from the kettle, if necessary. Remove from the heat and cover with a clean towel. Leave for 5 minutes and then stir in the remaining butter.

What goes with what ...
Serve the quail on a bed of tomato rice. You must have cold Greek yoghurt with this dish, and a glass of Notios red.

wedding pilaff

For once, the name is accurate! This is a pilaff that you serve at a wedding. It is a long and complex dish that usually takes its place among a host of other dishes.

SERVES 15 PEOPLE AS PART OF
A BUFFET

1kg chuck steak in one piece

500g beef bones

5 bay leaves

5 cloves of garlic, peeled.

About 4 litres water

1 shoulder of goat or lamb
    (including the neck fillet)

1 guinea fowl

500g leeks, roughly chopped

500g carrots, peeled

500g shallots, peeled

1 head of Lahano (or 500g spring
    greens or Savoy cabbage)

500g courgettes, roughly chopped

About 300g short-grain rice

100g ricotta cheese

Juice of 2 lemons

50g butter

Sea salt and freshly ground black
    pepper

1 Take a vast pot and add to it the piece of beef, the bones, bay leaves and the garlic. Cover with water. Bring to simmering point and cook for 1 hour.

2 Add the whole shoulder of goat or lamb and cook for a further hour. Then add the whole guinea fowl, together with the leeks, carrots, shallots and the whole Lahano or cabbage. Cook on for 30 minutes.

3 Add the courgettes and cook on for 10 more minutes.

4 Take the pot off the heat and place the meats on separate trays. Discard the beef bones and use a slotted spoon to remove the vegetables and put them on a separate tray.

5 Take the broth in the pot and bring it to the boil; skim thoroughly. Reduce it by a third.

6 Measure the broth and for every 30ml, measure out 2 teaspoons of rice. Cook the rice gently in the broth until all the liquid has been absorbed. Take it off the heat and stir in the ricotta cheese and lemon juice.

7 Melt the butter in a pan until brown and nutty and pour it over the rice. Stir it in and season to taste.

What goes with what ...
Carve the meats onto platters and serve them alongside the rice and vegetables. Everything should be at room temperature. As you are at a wedding, you should drink too much with this dish! ... Perhaps Megas Oenos.

πιτσουνι γεμιστο με χυλοπιτες στο φουρνο

squab pigeon with chestnuts and tagliatelle

When the holy days were coming, my parents would send us children to stay with my uncle, who was a General in the army and lived in Theba to the North of Athens. He was a crack shot and the migrating pigeons were no match for him. His household was where I first tried this dish.

4 squab pigeon

Juice and zest of 2 lemons

4 heaped teaspoons fresh thyme
    leaves

500g calves kidneys

250g chicken livers

150g plain flour, seasoned with
    salt and pepper

250ml olive oil

250ml red wine

250g shallots, finely chopped

2 bunches of spring onions, finely
    chopped

3 cloves of garlic, peeled and
    finely chopped

4 heaped tablespoons finely
    chopped fresh mint

100g butter

750g cooked chestnuts (either
    vacuum packed or tinned, from
    supermarkets)

300g ripe plum tomatoes

500ml chicken stock

500g hilopites (Greek egg
    tagliatelle)

150g grated feta cheese

Sea salt and freshly ground black
    pepper

1 Preheat your oven to 170°C/325°F/Gas 3. Wash the squabs well and rub them with 50ml of the olive oil, the juice from one lemon, the lemon zest from both lemons and the thyme leaves. Season the birds.

2 Cut the calves kidneys into chunks that are roughly the same size as the chicken livers. Roll both in the seasoned flour.

3 Heat 100ml of olive oil in a large frying pan and start by cooking the kidneys for a few minutes on either side. Remove and drain on kitchen paper.

4 Repeat the process with the chicken livers, but note that they will only need half as long in the pan. When the livers are cooked, drain and discard the surplus oil.

5 Deglaze the pan with the red wine and cook down until syrupy. Pour it off into a jug.

6 Add half the remaining olive oil to the pan and sauté the shallots, spring onions and garlic for a few minutes until soft. Take off the heat. Add the livers, kidneys, butter, the chopped mint and the reduced wine. Crush the chestnuts roughly and add them to the pan. Mix together well and use to stuff the squabs.

7 Lay out three square sheets of baking parchment, one on top of another – they should be about 25 x 25cm.

8 Place a stuffed squab in the centre of each sheet, top with a quarter of the tomatoes and sprinkle with the remaining olive oil. Make into neat parcels and secure the paper with string. Place on a roasting tray and cook in the oven for 2¹/₂ hours. To check if they are ready, plunge a meat thermometer into the parcel at the thickest point: it should read between 75–80°C/167–176°F.

9 To finish the dish, cut open the parcels and spoon the juices and the stuffing into the roasting tray. Keep the pigeons warm under some foil. Add the tagliatelle and the feta cheese to the dish and mix well. If it seems too dry, add a little chicken stock. Put back into the oven for 10–15 minutes. The noodles should be cooked, but still quite "sloppy".

What goes with what ...
Serve the birds on top of the tagliatelle and stuffing mixture, and accompany the dish with Amethystos red, a blend of Cabernet Sauvignon and Merlot that gives a splendid softness.

salads

THE TERM "GREEK SALAD" IS ONE OF THE MOST ABUSED IN THE WORLD.

GREECE HAS A LARGE RANGE OF INTERESTING AND NOVEL SALADS, NEARLY

ALL OF WHICH REQUIRE THE INGREDIENTS TO BE WILTED FIRST, PLUS SEVERAL

INTERESTING VEGETABLE ACCOMPANIMENTS. THESE RECIPES ARE DESIGNED

FOR FOUR PEOPLE, PLEASE FEEL FREE TO SCALE THEM UP OR DOWN.

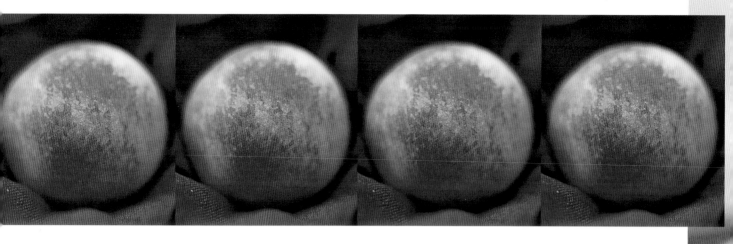

πρασινες πιπεριες
με ροδακινα

salad of green peppers and peaches

This is a novel configuration of sweetness and tang, and goes well with cold meats, rich salamis or pastourma (cured meat).

1.5kg green peppers
150ml extra virgin olive oil
1 tablespoon brown sugar
1kg large, ripe (but not overripe) peaches
3 dessertspoons cumin seeds
2 teaspoons cayenne pepper
1 dessertspoon lemon juice
Sea salt and freshly ground black pepper

1 Preheat your oven to 180°C/350°F/Gas 4.

2 Wash, core and quarter the green peppers. Spread the peppers out on a shallow roasting tray and sprinkle them with half of the olive oil and the sugar. Season well and ensure the pieces are well coated. Roast in the oven for about 45–60 minutes. Halfway through the cooking time, you will notice that the edges of some of the peppers have turned brown and acquired a crunchy edge. Give them another good mix in, so that they do not burn and stick to the bottom of the pan. Remove from the oven and allow to cool.

3 Take a sharp knife and peel and pit the peaches. Slice them into chunky wedges. Put them in a large salad bowl and mix them with the cooled green peppers.

4 Toss the cumin seeds in a dry pan over a medium heat until they start popping. Do not let them turn brown as they will taste bitter. Crush the toasted cumin in a pestle, then mix it with the cayenne pepper and sprinkle the resulting coarse powder over the salad. Add the remaining olive oil and the lemon juice. Stir all the ingredients well, check the seasoning and adjust, then serve.

σαλατα με κρεμμυδακια και θυμαρισιο μελι

salad of shallots and thyme honey

Do try and use the delicious Greek thyme honey. The floral notes complement the sweet shallots.

1kg small shallots, peeled
200g cauliflower in florets
200g broccoli in florets
200g asparagus, peeled and cut
  into 1cm pieces
100g rocket, washed

DRESSING
100ml extra virgin olive oil
50ml white wine vinegar
130g thyme honey
2 tablespoons Dijon mustard
1 dessertspoon finely chopped
  parsley
1 tablespoon black sesame seeds
Sea salt and freshly ground black
  pepper

1 Cook the small shallots in boiling, salted water for 15–20 minutes. Drain them and add them to a large salad bowl.
2 Blanch the cauliflower, broccoli and asparagus in boiling, salted water for 2 minutes. Drain, plunge into cold water and drain again. Add to the bowl, then add the rocket and mix together.
3 Prepare the dressing by blending the olive oil, vinegar, honey and mustard in a liquidizer or food processor. Taste and season carefully.
4 Toss the vegetables in the dressing and finally, sprinkle on the parsley and sesame seeds. Serve at room temperature.

maroulosalata

The classic lettuce salad from the island of Cos ... and everywhere else in Greece.

150ml extra virgin olive oil

2 tablespoons white wine vinegar

1 Cos lettuce, shredded very finely

1 bunch of spring onions, finely chopped including the green parts

3 tablespoons finely chopped dill weed

Sea salt and freshly ground black pepper

1 Mix the oil and vinegar together in a bowl. Add salt and pepper to taste.

2 Combine the ingredients and toss with the dressing. Serve as soon as possible; this salad should taste crunchy and not soggy.

vinegar-poached courgettes

These courgettes are useful whenever you want to add an acidic touch when serving any dish.

8 courgettes
500ml good-quality red wine
     vinegar
About 100ml water
75ml extra virgin olive oil
1 tablespoon finely chopped fresh
     mint
Sea salt and freshly ground black
     pepper

1 Cut the courgettes in half lengthways. With a small spoon, remove the seeds and then cut the courgettes into long batons of about 1cm square by 4cm long.

2 Put the courgette batons into a non-reactive saucepan and add the vinegar. Then add enough water to barely cover them. Bring to the boil and then reduce to simmering point. Cook for about 10 minutes until the vegetables are soft, but not falling apart by which time they should have absorbed all the liquid.

3 Remove them with a slotted spoon and place them in a large bowl. Dress them while warm with the olive oil, mint and plenty of coarse sea salt and black pepper.

warm salad of artichokes

Frying the artichokes in batter emphasizes their nutty taste. Very yummy.

6 globe artichokes
3 lemons
1 litre groundnut oil for frying

BATTER
100g self raising flour
1 large egg
60g grated Kefalotiri cheese (or
     substitute Pecorino cheese)
Sea salt and freshly ground black
     pepper

radishes and lemon mayonnaise
     to serve

1 To prepare the artichokes, first cut off the stem to leave about 3cm and then peel the remaining stem. Take off the outer two rings of leaves and slice the artichoke across to separate the base from the leaves. Trim it back to reveal the hairy "choke" in the centre of the bud. Remove it carefully with a teaspoon. Each artichoke must be rubbed over with half a lemon and then kept in water which has had a squeeze of lemon added to it. The acidulated water stops them oxidizing and going black.

2 Put the artichokes in a large pot of boiling water and blanch them for about 7 minutes. Remove them from the water and dip them into icy water until the batter is ready.

3 Preheat the groundnut oil in your deep fryer to 200°C/400°F.

4 Make the batter in a bowl. Sift the flour into the bowl. Add the egg and cheese, and whisk it until you've got a smooth batter. You are aiming for a batter that is the consistency of thick cream. If the mixture is too stiff, add a little water. Season well.

5 Halve the artichokes lengthwise. Dip them in the batter and cook in the hot oil for about 3 minutes depending on the size of the artichokes until the batter is crisp and golden. Pat dry with kitchen paper.

6 Serve with plenty of breakfast radishes and lemony mayonnaise.

horta with ladolemono sauce

χορτα με λαδολεμονο

This is the classic Greek "greens" dish. The leaves taste of iron and the lemony sauce makes the perfect foil.

200g beetroot leaves or substitute
   red Swiss chard leaves
200g rocket
100g mustard leaves
100g green dandelion leaves, if
   unavailable, use rocket
100g root spinach
Sea salt and freshly ground black
   pepper

SAUCE
40ml lemon juice
100ml extra virgin olive oil
Sea salt and freshly ground black
   pepper

1 To make the ladolemono sauce, whisk the lemon juice with the olive oil in a bowl until the two ingredients are amalgamated. Season to taste.
2 Blanch all the leaves in a pot of boiling, salted water for 5 minutes. Drain them in a colander and squeeze them with kitchen tongs. Toss with the ladolemono sauce and add extra salt and pepper, if necessary.

σαλατα με χορτα,
μαυροματικα
φασολια και ντοματες

salad of mixed greens, black-eyed beans and plum tomatoes

A complex mixture of tastes and textures that makes this salad satisfying – a long way from the limp lettuce of times past!

250g beetroot leaves (or
   substitute red Swiss chard
   leaves)
250g large-leaf spinach
250g green dandelion leaves (if
   unavailable, use rocket)
250g fresh methi leaves (from
   Asian stores; if unavailable, use
   watercress including the stems)
500g black-eyed beans
12 small new potatoes, peeled
6 small courgettes, left whole
6 plum tomatoes
1 bunch of spring onions, trimmed
Sea salt and freshly ground black
   pepper

DRESSING
250ml extra virgin olive oil
Juice of 2 lemons
2 tablespoons lukewarm water
1 teaspoon English mustard
Sea salt and freshly ground black
   pepper

1 Wash all the leaves carefully and leave them in a large bowl or bucket covered with water.
2 Take a large casserole and add the black-eyed beans and 5 litres of water. Bring to the boil and cook with the lid on for 1 hour, then add the new potatoes and salt.
3 After 5 more minutes, add the courgettes and after 10 minutes drain the leaves and add them. Cook for 5 minutes and drain carefully.
4 To serve, put the olive oil, lemon juice, warm water, mustard and salt and pepper into a jar with a lid. Place the warm salad in a large bowl. Cut the plum tomatoes into quarters and chop the spring onions including the green parts. Add them to the bowl and mix well.
5 Shake the jar until the dressing turns cloudy and pour it over the salad. Serve at room temperature.

pickled green peppers and pan fried feta

These piperonia can be made at home or bought in tins. You need the pickled, long, green, mild chilli peppers and olive oil. Check the seasoning: it is delicious with dishes such as lentils with lakerda or cannellini beans. Don't forget to warm up plenty of sour dough bread!

50ml olive oil

250g good feta cheese, cut into long, triangular batons

50g flour

150g Greek black olives (choose the ones which have been bottled or tinned in olive oil)

Pickled green peppers (page 181)

75ml extra virgin olive oil

Sea salt and freshly ground black pepper

1 Heat the ordinary olive oil in a frying pan.

2 Roll each narrow wedge of feta in flour and then pan fry it for about 2 or 3 minutes until the flour coating is turning golden. Lift the feta out carefully with a palette knife (it can be fragile) and transfer it to a serving plate.

3 Arrange the feta with the olives and some of the pickled green peppers on a plate – the exact balance between ingredients is up to you.

Sprinkle lavishly with the extra virgin olive oil and season to taste.

spinach salad with yoghurt

A dish where the rich mineral flavours of the spinach are balanced by acidic yoghurt.

1kg large-leaf spinach

3 spring onions, trimmed and very finely chopped (including the green parts)

2 cloves of garlic, peeled and crushed

2 tablespoons extra virgin olive oil

1 tablespoon lemon juice

1 bunch of mint

400g yoghurt

50g melted butter

Sea salt and freshly ground black pepper

1 Wash the spinach thoroughly and shred it very finely.

2 Sauté the spring onions and the garlic in the olive oil for 2–3 minutes until they are softening.

3 Add the spinach and season with salt and pepper. Mix well and cook briefly until the spinach dries out a little.

4 Allow the spinach mixture to cool and add the lemon juice. Strip the mint leaves from their stems and add them to the pan.

5 Mix the greens and the yoghurt together in a bowl. Check and adjust the seasoning with salt, pepper and lemon juice.

6 Just before serving, pour the melted butter over the finished dish and serve at room temperature.

cheese
and bakery

THERE ARE OVER 300 ARTISANAL CHEESES IN GREECE, SOME OF THEM

NOTABLE. CHEESE IS MOST FREQUENTLY EATEN WHEN COOKED, RATHER

THAN COLD FROM A CHEESEBOARD AS IN BRITAIN. THERE IS ALSO

QUITE A SPECTACULAR ARRAY OF BREADS AND PASTRIES.

homemade filo

σπιτικο φυλλο

If you can make pasta successfully, then you can also make filo. It is something of a revelation to discover how much nicer homemade pastry tastes than shop-bought. Always keep filo cool and damp when you are working with it.

1kg white pasta flour (grade 00)
1 dessertspoon salt
About 250ml water
1 tablespoon white wine vinegar
50ml extra virgin olive oil

1 Take a large mixing bowl and sift the flour and salt together. Make a well in the centre and add the water and vinegar.

2 Work the dough until smooth. Then add the olive oil, a little at a time, kneading as it is absorbed until the dough is shiny and elastic. Wrap and refrigerate until quite cold.

3 Use a pasta machine to roll out long, ultra-thin sheets.

layered cheese pie

πιτα με ανθοτυρο

A cheese pie that originated in Asia Minor. It is hard to find a suitable name for this in English as it is not a streudel, or a mille feuille, or even a pie really ... and cheese "stack" doesn't seem to work! Try making it yourself and then call it whatever you will. It'll still be delicious.

50ml extra virgin olive oil plus
    extra for brushing
1kg (2 packets) filo
50ml melted butter
500ml whole milk
2 medium eggs

FILLING
6 medium eggs
500g cottage cheese
500g good feta cheese (Greek, oak
    barrel matured, if possible)
50ml extra virgin olive oil
2 tablespoons chopped fresh dill
2 tablespoons chopped fresh mint
Sea salt and freshly ground black
    pepper

1 To make the filling, take a mixing bowl and a hand mixer and beat the six eggs in it.

2 Add the cottage cheese, feta and extra virgin olive oil. Snip the dill and the mint leaves finely with scissors and add to the mixture. Check the seasoning, which will vary depending on how salty your feta is, and adjust to suit.

3 Preheat your oven, which probably means as hot as you can.

4 Brush a baking sheet with extra virgin olive oil and add a sheet of filo. (Keep your filo under a damp cloth, if you let it dry out it will become hard to handle.) Brush with melted butter and add another sheet of filo.

5 Add a 1cm thick layer of the cheese mixture, extending to the edge of the sheet. Then add another two oiled sheets of filo, and then more mixture. Repeat until all the filling is used up and then top with two final buttered sheets of filo.

6 Make a diamond pattern of deep cuts through the top sheet of filo. Beat the milk, any remaining butter, the extra virgin olive oil and the two eggs together and pour the mixture gently over the top of the stack. Allow it to rest and soak up the liquid for 15 minutes.

7 Put the pie in the oven for 7–8 minutes, or until it has got some colour, and then turn the oven down to 150°C/300°F/Gas 2 and continue to bake for about 20 minutes.

spinach roll with feta

Genuine Greek filo is never very crisp – most people make their own – but ready-made filo will make a crisp pastry. It's a matter of taste as to which you prefer. Let the spanakopita cool down and eat them either with Greek yoghurt or in the summer with one of the crispier salads.

MAKES 12 PASTRIES

150g butter

100ml olive oil

175g leeks, washed thoroughly, trimmed and cut into 4cm pieces

500g large-leaf spinach, washed carefully, drained and shredded (including the stems)

3 heaped tablespoons finely chopped fresh dill (including the stems)

400g Greek feta, crumbled

2 medium eggs

40ml whole milk

1kg filo pastry (if using shop-bought, you want to end up with sheets of 18 x 30cm)

Freshly ground black pepper and very little sea salt as the feta is already salted

1 Heat 50g butter and 50ml olive oil in a saucepan. Add the leeks and cover and cook over a medium heat until the leeks are soft, but not coloured, about 20 minutes. (You will need to stir the leeks occasionally to prevent them from sticking.) When the leeks are ready, remove the pan from the heat and let them cool down completely.

2 Preheat your oven to 180°C/350°F/Gas 4.

3 Put the spinach into a large mixing bowl. Add the dill, feta, the remaining olive oil, pepper, salt (if any is needed) and one beaten egg.

4 Add the leeks and mix the filling together thoroughly with your hands.

5 In a pan, melt the remaining butter and get a pastry brush. Make an egg-wash with the remaining egg and the milk.

6 Remove the filo from the fridge and cover it with a damp cloth – you are now ready to assemble the dish!

7 Take one sheet of filo and brush it first with melted butter and then with eggwash. Then put another sheet of filo on the top of it. Repeat the coat of melted butter and eggwash. Spread about 150g of the spinach mixture over the filo, leaving a clean edge of 1½cm all around for folding. Sprinkle some eggwash over the spinach mixture and roll the filo up like a long, fat cigar, folding the end inside to ensure a seal.

8 Repeat and place each roll on a baking sheet. Carry on making the rolls until you have used up all the spinach mix.

9 Bake in the oven for 20–25 minutes. The rolls are ready when the filo has become a light brown colour.

κολοκυθοπιτα ηπειρου
vegetable marrow
and feta cheese pie

In September as the weather gets a little cooler on Epirus, the grazing improves and with it the milk yield increases. This is the season when most farmers' wives make the first butter for several months. It also brings the ripening of huge vegetable marrows and these two seasonal ingredients come together in this splendid little pie. Although you can make one large pie, the small, individual pies are more stylish. The perfect tin is a 10cm wide mini flan case. They come in two parts: the fluted ring and the separate base plate.

MAKES 4 INDIVIDUAL PIES

800g vegetable marrow

Table salt

1 tablespoon finely chopped fresh
   basil leaves

2 tablespoons olive oil

1 dessertspoon unsalted butter
   plus extra for greasing

2 medium eggs

150g feta cheese

Flour for rolling out

500g packet of puff pastry (try
   and get one of the "deluxe"
   supermarket puff pastries,
   which have a higher butter
   content; the ingredients label
   will guide you)

Sea salt and freshly ground black
   pepper

1 Peel the marrow and cut it into quarters lengthways. Deseed carefully, and then grate into a colander using the largest holes of a cheese grater. Sprinkle with a light dusting of table salt and put a plate on top with a weight on top of that. Leave for 2 hours or overnight to draw out as much water as possible.

2 Mix the basil in a bowl with the oil and the butter, and one of the eggs, beaten. Then crumble in the feta cheese carefully. Season with freshly ground black pepper, but do not add salt: there will already be enough in the feta and the marrow.

3 Take the marrow from the colander, give it one last squeeze, and add it to the mixture. Mix gently – you do not want to end up with a mush.

4 On a floured surface, roll out the puff pastry. Take four loose-bottomed flan tins and grease them with a smear of butter. Make pastry circles that overlap the tin edges by a generous margin; you will need plenty of spare pastry to crimp the edges.

5 Cut 10cm circles of pastry for the lids. Fill each pie with a quarter of the mixture. Beat the second egg in a cup to use as a "glue" to seal the base and lid together and for glazing. Add each lid and bring the edge up, crimping it in a roll as you would a Cornish pasty, and gluing all in place with egg. Cut a small slit in the lids to allow the steam to escape. Brush the whole pies with more beaten egg and sprinkle with a few crystals of sea salt. Put in the fridge and rest for 20 minutes, or longer if that suits your dinner party plans.

6 Put a thick baking sheet into the oven and preheat the oven to 180°C/350°F/Gas 4. Put the pies straight onto the hot baking sheet to cook the bottoms. Then after 30 minutes, lift the pies (on their little tin bases) out of the rings and put them back in the oven for 15 more minutes to brown the sides.

crisp cheese squares
τυροπιτα τριφτη θρακης

These cheesy nibbles are very rich, so resist the temptation to make them larger. When cool, they store well in a sealed box, where they will keep for several weeks.

MAKES BETWEEN 30 AND 40
SMALL BISCUITS

115g butter
100ml olive oil
130ml milk
1¹/₂ dessertspoons baking
   powder
60g grated Kefalotiri cheese (or
   substitute a tangy Pecorino)
60g grated feta cheese
2 teaspoons salt
400g plain flour

1 Preheat your oven to 180°C/350°F/Gas 4 and line baking sheets with baking parchment. You will need three domestic sized baking sheets for this quantity of dough.

2 Use an electric mixer or a large bowl and a wooden spoon, and start by beating the butter until fluffy. Lower the speed and add the olive oil gradually, mixing the two together.

3 Add the milk, at which stage, if well beaten, the mixture will resemble mayonnaise. Then add the baking powder, the two cheeses and the salt. You may use less salt if the cheeses are particularly salty.

4 Add about a third of the flour and then as the dough starts to come together, transfer to a work surface and add the remaining flour. Work it into the dough by hand until you have a soft dough.

5 Roll the dough out on a floured surface until 5mm thick and cut into small squares of about 2cm on each side. Arrange them on the baking parchment. (They do not spread, so they can be placed quite closely together.) Bake for 15–25 minutes until a light golden brown. Remove and cool them down on a rack.

saffron and cottage cheese tartlets

This is a very more-ish little pastry that comes from Thraki. The tartlets are best made in 8cm individual flan dishes, preferably those thin, metal ones with removable base plates.

MAKES ENOUGH FOR 10
TARTLETS (AND HALF THE PASTRY
IS LEFT OVER TO FREEZE)

100ml clarified butter
100g unsalted butter
100g sugar
2 medium eggs
450g soft white plain flour (like 00
    pasta flour)

FILLING

4 strands of saffron
75ml sweet white wine
1kg Ricotta cheese
1 whole medium egg (plus
    1 additional egg yolk for
    eggwash)
1 dessertspoon ground cinnamon

1 Put the saffron strands in a glass to soak in the wine.

2 To make the dough, put both kinds of butter into a mixing bowl (reserve a very small amount of the clarified butter to grease the flan tins) and add the sugar. Start to mix the ingredients together with a wooden spoon or a hand-held mixer on slow. Gradually add the eggs.

3 To quote my mum: "then add the flour slowly, slowly" until you have an elastic dough. Mix it well, but it needs very little kneading. It should be soft. Put it into the fridge in a container to firm up, which will take 30 minutes.

4 Preheat your oven to 180°C/350°F/Gas 4.

5 Grease the flan tins and roll out the chilled pastry to $^{1}/_{2}$cm thick. Use a 10cm saucer to cut out circles and then line each tin using your fingers to press the dough well into the fluted sides and corners.

6 In a mixing bowl combine the cheese, the whole egg and the saffron flavoured wine. Divide the mixture among the tartlets. Brush the top of each one with eggwash and sprinkle with cinnamon.

7 Bake for 30 minutes, then remove from the oven. Leave to cool before attempting to remove the tartlets from their cases.

τηγανιτα ανθοτυροπιτακια με μελι
cottage cheese savouries with honey

These are small, sweet and savoury, cheesy, crunchy, soft, sort of ... after or before dinner treats.

MAKES 10–20 INDIVIDUAL
NIBBLES

500g cottage cheese
60g sugar
1 litre groundnut oil
200g runny honey

BATTER
1 large egg
200ml milk
100–125g self-raising flour (use
just enough to make the
batter)

1 First, make the batter by beating the egg in a large bowl and whisking in the milk. Then add flour a little at a time, whisking as you go. When you have a thick batter, you are ready to proceed. Cover the bowl with cling film and put in the fridge while you make the cheese balls.

2 Turn the cottage cheese out into a clean tea towel and drain it well; squeeze dry. Mix it in a bowl with the sugar. Shape into spheres about 2cm in diameter.

3 Heat the oil in a pan and when it is hot but not smoking, coat the cheese balls in batter. Deep-fry them a few at a time for 3–4 minutes until they are golden and the batter coating is crisp. Transfer them to a tray lined with kitchen paper to cool down a little.

4 Drizzle with honey and serve.

basic bread dough

καθημερινο ασπρο ψωμι

Even if you have never made your own bread before, you should consider trying now. Nothing is as gratifying, appetizing, satisfying and as yummy as your own bread.

MAKES 2 LOAVES

1 tablespoon instant yeast
600ml water (at blood heat)
1 teaspoon sugar
1.1kg strong, white flour
30g salt
Olive oil to grease the bowl
Butter to grease the baking sheet
1 egg, beaten

1 In a bowl, dissolve the yeast in a little of the water with the sugar and wait until it is frothy.

2 Mix the flour and salt together on a work surface to form a heap, then make a well in the centre. Add the rest of the water to the yeast mixture. Draw the flour together by pouring the liquid into the middle of the flour and work by hand into a dough.

3 Knead the dough. Remember that you are "stretching" the gluten within the flour and that is what you should do with the dough. After 7–8 minutes the feel of the dough will change (in some magical way it stops feeling sticky). Whether you are working by hand or with a machine, the dough is ready when you spread a little out between your hands and it stretches to a thin skin without breaking.

4 Oil a bowl and put the dough into it. Cover it with a cloth and put it to rise. If you leave it inside an airing cupboard, the job takes 1–2 hours. In the fridge, it may take a day or two.

5 When the dough has doubled in size, return it to the work surface and knead until you have knocked the puffiness out of it.

6 To make a plain loaf, continue as follows. Form the dough into two long, oval loaves (like miniature versions of those bakery loaves called "Bloomers"). Put them onto a greased baking sheet and set aside to prove (rise) for 45 minutes.

7 Preheat your oven to 230°C/450°F/Gas 8, which probably means "as hot as possible"!

8 When the loaves have risen, paint the tops with eggwash. Then make a series of knife cuts across each loaf on the diagonal, about 1cm deep.

9 Bake in the oven for 35–40 minutes, reducing the heat to 200°C/400°F/Gas 6 for the last 25 minutes. The bread is cooked when you can tap the bottom with your finger and it sounds hollow. There is no substitute for experience in judging this; the sooner you start baking regularly, the sooner you'll be doing this confidently.

10 When the bread is cooked, leave to cool on a rack before slicing. Warm bread is delicious, but hot bread is horrid: it has not had a chance for the structure inside to firm up, or a crust to harden.

traditional cheese bread

This is a very self-indulgent recipe and the finished loaf is almost sticky in the middle.

MAKES 5 SMALL LOAVES

350g good-quality feta cheese, crumbled

60ml extra virgin olive oil

1/2 teaspoon coarsely ground black pepper

1 tablespoon finely chopped fresh mint

1/3 quantity Basic Bread Dough (page 141)

Flour for dusting

1 medium egg, beaten with 1 tablespoon of milk for eggwash

1 Preheat the oven to 180°C/350°F/Gas 4.

2 Knead the cheese, oil, pepper and mint into the dough. If the dough is sticky, use some more flour. Divide the dough into five equal pieces and give them a round shape. Use your hands to make them a bit flatter, i.e. like the typical Arabic bread.

3 Place the pieces on a thick baking tray which has been slightly floured. Cover with a damp cloth and let them rise at room temperature. This will take 40–60 minutes.

4 When the loaves have risen, make indentations all over the surface with your small finger, glaze them with eggwash and put them in the oven. Bake for 20–30 minutes.

5 Leave the bread on a rack to cool down before eating as it can be heavy when hot.

"Don't buy an egg from him, it won't have a yolk inside!"

(On the subject of dishonest shopkeepers)

ψωμι γεμιστο με
σπανακι και τυρι

bread stuffed
with spinach and cheese

This is a very tasty bread which also looks good when sliced.

MAKES 4 SMALL LOAVES

500g spinach, washed and shaken
    dry, then finely shredded
250g bulb fennel (including the
    leaves), finely sliced
4 heaped tablespoons finely
    chopped dill
1 bunch spring onions, trimmed
    and finely chopped including
    the green parts
500g feta cheese, grated
80ml extra virgin olive oil
1 quantity of risen Basic Bread
    Dough (page 141)
200g butter
Sea salt and freshly ground black
    pepper

BECHAMEL SAUCE

600ml milk
90g butter
90g plain flour
2 medium eggs, beaten

1 First, make a very thick Béchamel mixture. Set the milk to heat in a saucepan. Then melt the butter in a deep frying pan. Stir in the flour and cook the paste gently without letting it colour.

2 Add the hot milk a little at a time, stirring it in well so that each batch is completely absorbed before you add more milk. Cool to room temperature while you prepare the filling.

3 Take a bowl and mix together the spinach, fennel, dill, spring onions, feta and olive oil thoroughly.

4 Beat the two eggs into the cool Béchamel.

5 Combine the Béchamel sauce and the spinach mixtures. Check and adjust the seasoning. (It will already be quite salty with the feta.)

6 Preheat your oven to 180°C/350°F/Gas 4.

7 Divide the dough into four equal parts. Take each one and roll it out to form a 30cm square about 5mm thick. Spread each dough square with a quarter of the filling, leaving a clear 3cm margin on all four sides.

8 Roll the dough and stuffing up like a Swiss roll to form a "baguette". Crimp the two ends tightly shut with the tines of a fork and fold them underneath.

9 Melt the butter and pour into four roasting dishes. Brush each loaf all over with melted butter and then sit them in the remaining melted butter in each of the dishes.

10 Bake for 50 minutes, then remove the roasting dishes from the oven and wait until the loaves have cooled down completely before taking them out and cutting them up.

κουζουνια με ορτυκια
bread with quails

This recipe looks bizarre and unusual, but it is worth persevering.

MAKES 1 LOAF

75ml extra virgin olive oil

Basic Bread Dough (page 141)

3 boned quail (either from your
supermarket, or ask your
butcher; or failing all else,
substitute boneless chicken
thighs opened out!)

5 pickled, mild green chillies

2 red onions, peeled and sliced
very thinly

2 plum tomatoes, sliced

2 tablespoons fresh thyme,
chopped

50ml hot milk

Sea salt and freshly ground black
pepper

1 Preheat your oven to 200°C/400°F/Gas 6.

2 Use a little of the oil to grease a shallow round cake tin, about 20cm across x 5cm deep.

3 Divide the dough into two pieces, one slightly larger than the other; the proportions should be roughly one third to two thirds. Roll the larger one out until it is between 1.5 and 2cm thick. Place the dough in the cake tin (its edges should hang over the sides).

4 Arrange the quail, chillies, onions, tomatoes and thyme over the surface of the dough. Drizzle with the remaining oil and season well. Brush the edge of the dough with cold water.

5 Roll out the second piece of dough (once again, it shouldn't be more than 2cm thick) and use it to cover the stuffing. Brush the edge of the "lid" with cold water as well and stick the join together by pressing with your fingers.

6 Put the bread to one side to prove (rise) for 20 minutes and meanwhile, preheat your oven to 200°C/400°F/Gas 6.

7 Prick the surface of the bread all over with a skewer to let the steam out during cooking. Brush with hot milk and bake for about 25 minutes.

8 Put a baking tray in the oven to heat while you carefully remove the loaf from the top. Brush the surface with hot milk and put it back into the oven onto the hot tray. Bake for a further 20 minutes to crispen up the crust.

μπουγατσα πελοπονυησου
peloponnese bread

This is a typical Peloponnesian bread recipe that is eaten warm or cold, when you will find that it gets crunchier.

MAKES 1 LARGE LOAF

500g strong white bread flour

220ml extra virgin olive oil plus
extra for greasing

75ml white wine

Juice of 1 lemon

145g sugar

1 teaspoon cinnamon

$1/4$ teaspoon ground cloves

1 teaspoon bicarbonate of soda

1 dessertspoon sesame seeds

1 Preheat your oven to 220°C/425°F/Gas 7.

2 Put the flour in a mixing bowl. Add the olive oil and rub the two ingredients in together.

3 In another bowl, mix together the wine, lemon juice, sugar, cinnamon, cloves and bicarbonate of soda. Add them to the flour and knead well until you have a soft dough.

4 Grease a baking tray and sprinkle it with half the sesame seeds. Shape the dough into a loaf with your hands and put it on the baking tray. Sprinkle over the remaining sesame seeds and use a fork to make a few holes in the top.

5 Put the tray in the oven and bake for about 1 hour. The loaf is ready when you tap the bottom and it sounds hollow. Cool on a rack.

curly bread-sticks

To make good sticks the dough should be full of air bubbles and feel like a "soft bottom". My mother used to have them with her evening tea and cheese. In an airtight container they will keep for a couple of days.

1kg strong white bread flour

1 tablespoon coarse sea salt

200ml extra virgin olive oil

40g fresh yeast (or 1 tablespoon instant yeast dissolved in a little warm water with a pinch of sugar and left until frothy)

500ml "hand-hot" water

1 litre groundnut oil for frying

1 Put the flour, salt and olive oil into a large bowl and mix these ingredients together with your hands. If you are using fresh yeast, dissolve it in the water and add it slowly to the flour mix. Knead well for 15 minutes. The end result should be elastic (see the bread-making recipe on page 141).

2 Cover the bowl with a tea towel and let the dough rise. This will take about 1 hour if the temperature is about 20°C/68°F.

3 Preheat the oil in your deep fryer to 185°C/365°F.

4 "Knock back" the dough: this means kneading it again to break up any large bubbles. Cut it into walnut-sized pieces. Roll each piece between your hands until they are as long as shoelaces.

5 Fry the pieces, a few at a time for 2–3 minutes. They are ready when they come back to the surface and become a golden, fair colour. Remove and place them on kitchen paper to absorb any excess oil.

χιωτικα κουλουρακια
με ρακι

raki biscuits

These are little ring shaped, hard biscuits flavoured with raki (grappa from the island of Chios). When my mother used to make these cookies, she used half water and half raki to knead the dough, but my father always argued with her that water is for the sick people and so she should have used just raki!

MAKES 20–30 BISCUITS

500g strong white, plain flour
1/3 teaspoon baking powder
80g butter (at room temperature; plus a little extra to grease the baking tray)
80g sugar
Raki (you may substitute grappa, or make up a mixture of half spirit, half water)

1 Preheat your oven to 180°C/350°F/Gas 4.
2 Sift the flour with the baking powder into a large mixing bowl.
3 Cream the butter with the sugar in a separate bowl and add it to the flour.
4 Mix all the ingredients together well with your hands and start adding the raki (or the mixture of raki and water) until you have got a kneadable dough.
5 Shape the dough into small cookies with a hole in the middle (approximate weight 50g each) and place them on a lightly greased baking tray.
6 Put the tray in the centre of the oven and bake for 20 minutes. Transfer to a rack.

"*Sometimes you're pitta with a bottle, sometimes pitta alone*"

(pitta can translate as flat, and flat can translate as flat out or drunk)

desserts

AS WELL AS THE TRADITIONAL, HONEYED PASTRYWORK WITH ITS STRONG

MIDDLE-EASTERN INFLUENCES, HERE ARE SOME NEW AND QUITE AMBITIOUS

DISHES. GREEK DESSERTS ARE ALWAYS SWEET AND GO WELL WITH SOME OF

THE OUTSTANDING GREEK PUDDING WINES. LOOK OUT FOR THE DARK

MAVRODAPHNE AND THE HONEYED MUSCAT WINES –

PARTICULARLY THE MUSCAT FROM PATRAS.

cherry tomato glyko (spoon sweets)

ντοματουλες γλυκο

Glyko are traditionally eaten with a cup of strong coffee on awakening from an afternoon siesta. They are rich with honey and sugar, and provide an instant burst of energy as a pick-me-up. However, be warned: never put a spoon that you have sucked back into the jar of preserves. Aside from all the hygiene implications, there is an enzyme in saliva which will promptly crystallize all the syrup in the jar!

1.5kg cherry tomatoes (as firm
    as possible)
1.5 litres water
Juice of 2 lemons

SYRUP
1kg caster sugar
1 stick of cinnamon
8 cloves
8 whole allspice berries
200g blanched almonds
Grated zest of 1 lemon

1 Blanch the cherry tomatoes in boiling water for 10 seconds. Strain and peel off the skins.

2 Put 500ml of the water and the lemon juice in a bowl. Soak the tomatoes in it for 10–15 minutes.

3 Take the tomatoes out of the liquid and with a sharp knife, slit the bottom of each one; gently squeeze and shake out the seeds. Try and keep the tomatoes whole. When deseeded, put them back into the lemon juice and water to firm up even more for about 30 minutes.

4 Strain the tomatoes once more and arrange them to drain, cut side down, on kitchen paper.

5 Make the syrup by combining the remaining water with the sugar and spices. Boil vigorously, skimming off any scum from the surface, for about 10 minutes.

6 Take each tomato and slip a blanched almond into the slit. Put them all into the syrup and continue boiling for another 5 minutes. Remove the pot from the heat and allow to cool down.

7 Remove the tomatoes from the syrup with a slotted spoon and reserve while you bring the syrup back to the boil (add the lemon zest at this stage). Continue cooking until the syrup is thick enough to coat the back of a wooden spoon.

8 Remove from the heat and add the tomatoes. Allow to cool and then pot in sterilized jars as you would jam. Open after a month. Refrigerate after opening and they will keep for several weeks.

μελιτζανάκι γλυκό
baby aubergine glyko (spoon sweets)

Somewhat improbably, this glyko (which comes from Crete) is made from aubergines. These should ideally be small, whole aubergines, but if you cannot obtain them, simply cut larger ones into pieces that are about the size of an apricot.

1kg baby aubergines

2 lemons

About 30 peeled, blanched almonds (one for each aubergine or piece of aubergine)

2 cinnamon sticks

500g caster sugar

475g jar of Greek honey

5 cloves

1 Trim the stems from the baby aubergines and place them in a large bowl. Cover with water and add the juice of a lemon, which will help draw out any bitterness. Leave to soak overnight.

2 Empty the aubergines and the water into a large, non-reactive pan. Bring to the boil and leave to simmer, uncovered, for 15 minutes or until tender. Drain, and when cool enough to handle, push an almond into each piece of aubergine.

3 Put the cinnamon sticks into a large, non-reactive saucepan and add 500ml water. Bring to the boil, then reduce to a simmer. Leave to infuse for 30 minutes. Add the sugar and stir until dissolved.

4 Add the aubergines to the mixture and cook gently for about 10 minutes. Remove from the heat, cover and leave the aubergines to steep overnight.

5 Sterilize two x 500ml preserving jars, either with sterilizing solution or by running them through a dishwasher. (Remember to remove the rubber seals.)

6 Reheat the syrup and aubergines gently. Add the honey, the juice of the remaining lemon and the cloves. Cook until the syrup is thick enough to coat the back of a spoon. Pack into the preserving jars, seal and leave for at least three weeks before eating.

γαλακτομπουρικο με γλυκο κολοκυθι

pumpkin and custard tart

This dish is associated with Serres – a town in Northern Greece where they grow a lot of pumpkins.

MAKES 1 LARGE TART

1 x 500g packet of filo pastry
25g butter, melted

CUSTARD
900ml whole milk
125g sugar
65g butter
1 vanilla pod, split
125g semi-fine semolina
5 medium eggs
Zest and juice of 1 orange
2 tablespoons honey

PUMPKIN MOUSSE
500g pumpkin
200ml honey
50g butter
1 whole nutmeg, grated
3 medium eggs
80g sugar
100ml double cream

1 Preheat your oven to 180°C/350°F/Gas 4.

2 Line a flan dish with three layers of buttered filo and bake blind for 3 minutes. Remove from the oven and cool.

3 To make the custard, bring the milk to the boil in a pan with the sugar, butter and the vanilla pod. Then whisk in the semolina, stirring constantly.

4 Take the pan off the stove and allow to cool slightly (to avoid curdling the eggs). Whisk the eggs in a bowl and add them to the custard, whisking the mixture thoroughly as you go.

5 Fold in the orange zest and juice, and honey. Reserve.

6 To make the pumpkin mousse, peel and scoop out the middle of the pumpkin and cut it into chunks. Rub with the honey, butter and grated nutmeg and place in a roasting tray. Roast, uncovered, until the pumpkin is soft and caramelized. Leave to cool and turn the oven down to 150°C/300°F/Gas 2.

7 Put the pumpkin in a food processor or blender with the eggs, sugar and the cream. Whiz until you have a light mousse.

8 To assemble, fill the filo flan case three quarters full with the custard and then top with the pumpkin mixture. Bake in the oven for about 7 minutes until golden.

9 Leave to cool for 20 minutes to allow the tart to firm up. Serve lukewarm.

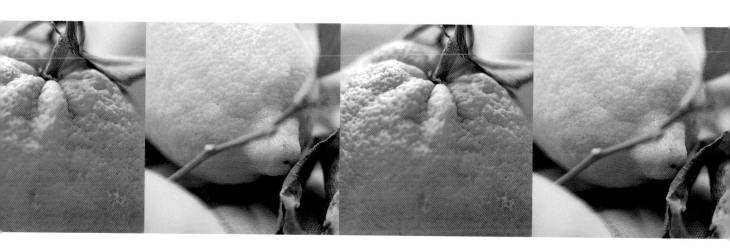

mixed nut pastries

καρυδόπιτα

It is hard to be exact with pastries, but this recipe will make about 36 short pastries when the rolls have been cut. The pastries must be soaked overnight in the syrup and then served with cold Greek yoghurt and yet more of the syrup!

MAKES ABOUT 36

200g shelled walnuts
160g shelled almonds
140g shelled pistachios
24 x 32.5 cm sheets shop-bought
    filo pastry
150g butter, melted
2 medium eggs, beaten to make
    eggwash

SYRUP

250g honey
400ml water
500g caster sugar
Zest and juice of 2 oranges
1 stick of cinnamon

1 Start by making the orange syrup. Boil the honey, water, sugar, orange zest and juice and cinnamon together in a pan until the syrup just begins to thicken. Stir, and leave the cinnamon in while you allow the syrup to cool.

2 To roast the nuts, preheat your oven to 200°C/400°F/Gas 6. Spread the nuts out on a baking sheet and give them 3–4 minutes in the hot oven. Watch them very carefully as ovens vary and they can easily burn. Remove and cool as soon as they are golden. Mix them together in a bowl and chop them finely. Divide the nuts into twelve portions and reduce the oven temperature to 150°C/300°F/Gas 2.

3 Lay out a sheet of filo, and brush it first with melted butter and then with eggwash. Cover with another sheet of filo and brush that too with melted butter and with eggwash.

4 Sprinkle one of the twelve portions of nuts over the sheet, leaving 1cm uncovered along the short edge to help make a seal.

5 Roll the pastry up like a long, thin Swiss roll, brushing with egg and butter at every full turn. Eggwash the outside and place the pastry on a baking sheet lined with baking parchment.

6 Repeat the filling and rolling process with the remaining pastry and filling.

7 Bake the rolls for 5 minutes, then turn the oven temperature down to 130°C/250°F/Gas ¹/₂. Continue baking until they become a golden brown.

8 Cut the rolls into 8cm lengths when cool and leave to soak in the syrup overnight. Serve with sharp, thick yoghurt. Do not refrigerate as they will solidify.

honey doughnuts

λουκουμαδες

This recipe makes about 60 dessertspoon sized doughnuts, which sounds like a lot... until you try them. They are very more-ish indeed.

MAKES ABOUT 60

1 teaspoon dried yeast
75ml warm water
70g sugar
440ml whole milk
70g unsalted butter
Pinch of salt
3 medium eggs
600g plain flour
Vegetable oil for deep frying
100g chopped pistachio nuts

SYRUP

375g honey
190ml water
375g caster sugar

1 In a bowl, dissolve the yeast in the warm water with a pinch of the sugar. Leave in a warm place to froth up.

2 Scald the milk and remove the pan from the heat.

3 Add the butter, sugar and salt to a large mixing bowl and pour over the hot milk. Stir together until all is dissolved and put to one side to cool.

4 Beat the eggs in a bowl until light and fluffy.

5 When the milk mixture has cooled to lukewarm, add the yeast mixture, and then the egg mixture.

6 Finally, work in the flour with a wooden spoon until you have a thick batter. Cover and rest at room temperature for at least an hour.

7 To make the syrup, boil the honey, water and sugar together in a pan for 5 minutes (use a large pan for this as the mixture froths up). Stir, skim and allow to cool.

8 Heat your oil to 170°C/338°F and deep-fry teaspoon sized balls of the mixture. Do not worry if they become gnarled; they will taste just as good as smooth ones.

9 When the doughnuts are golden, remove them with a slotted spoon and allow to drain thoroughly on kitchen paper.

10 Soak them in the warm honey syrup sprinkle, with chopped pistachio nuts and serve.

rice pudding with dried fruit compôte and roast pears

Rice pudding and fruit compôte are both old-fashioned concepts ... and none the worse for that!

SERVES 4

85g Greek short-grain or risotto
   rice
125ml water
300ml whole milk
1 vanilla pod
125g sugar
3 medium eggs
40g honey
A pinch of salt

DRIED FRUIT COMPOTE

250g dried apricots
250g dried figs
250g pitted prunes
125ml dark rum
2 litres water
1 x 6cm vanilla pod
1 x 6cm cinnamon stick
5 cloves
750g sugar

ROAST PEARS

4 hard pears
25g butter
150g soft brown sugar
2 dessertspoons powdered
   cinnamon

1 To make the rice pudding, put the rice, honey, salt and water into a large saucepan and bring to the boil. Add the lid and reduce the heat to simmering point. Cook until all the water has been absorbed by the rice.

2 Pour the milk into a double saucepan (bain-marie). Add the vanilla pod and part-cooked rice. Fill the bottom with boiling water and cook gently for about 8 minutes until the rice is tender.

3 Beat the sugar and eggs together in a bowl and pour the rice mixture into the eggs. Stir well. Return to the double saucepan and cook while stirring until the custard becomes thick. Cool the rice pudding and then remove the vanilla pod.

4 To make the compôte, soak the fruit in a large casserole with the rum and water for 1 hour. Add the vanilla pod, cinnamon stick, cloves and sugar. Cook on a low heat until the mixture reduces and becomes jam-like, then leave to cool. (Cover the bowl and the compôte will keep in the fridge for 4 or 5 days.)

5 Preheat the oven to 180°C/350°F/Gas 4.

6 Peel, core, and quarter the pears lengthways. Heat the butter in a roasting tray and add the pears. Shake the tin while the fruit browns.

7 Mix the sugar and cinnamon together in a bowl and sprinkle 1 dessertspoon over the pears. Roast the pears, uncovered, for 15 minutes or until they are soft.

8 The creamy rice pudding, rich fruit compôte and roast pears combine in a glamorous plateful. Sprinkle the second dessertspoon of cinnamon and sugar over the pudding.

"The cook and the poet are just alike. The art of each settles comfortably in the brain"

τάρτα αμυγδάλου
caramel and hazelnut tarts

These are delightful, caramelly, nutty little tarts. Serve with ice cream.

MAKES 4 TARTS

Butter for greasing the tins
4 teaspoons caster sugar
250g plain flour, plus extra for
   rolling out
A pinch of salt
250g butter
30ml cold water

FILLING

600g caster sugar
160ml water
600ml double cream
2 medium eggs
220g skinned, roasted hazelnuts

1 Preheat your oven to 180°C/350°F/Gas 4.

2 To make the pastry tart cases, first grease 4 x 10cm fluted tart tins (the ones with removable bases are best). Then combine the sugar, flour and salt in a mixing bowl and rub in the butter.

3 Add just enough cold water to bring the ingredients together as a smooth dough. Cover in cling film and refrigerate for 30 minutes to rest.

4 On a floured surface, roll out the pastry and use to line the tart tins. Line with baking parchment and baking beans and blind bake for 15 minutes, or until nicely browned.

5 To make the caramel filling, put the caster sugar and the water in a saucepan over a high heat and cook until you have a golden brown caramel in the pan. Stir constantly.

6 Remove the pan from the heat and allow the caramel to cool a little. Whisk in the cream, watching out for splattering. Set to one side.

7 Whisk the eggs in a bowl and then gradually pour in the caramel, whisking as you go.

8 Place a few hazelnuts into the bottom of each tart case and pour in the caramel mixture.

9 Bake for about 20 minutes, or until the mixture has set. Allow to cool and serve warm.

mustard ice cream

This may sound odd, but it tastes great – sweet and tangy at the same time.

MAKES ABOUT 1 LITRE

380ml double cream
350ml single cream
240ml whole milk
4 whole vanilla pods
Yolks of 10 medium eggs
250g caster sugar
100g smooth Dijon mustard
40g dark brown sugar
100g Greek honey

1 Take a large saucepan and add the two different creams and the milk to it. Split the vanilla pods carefully with a knife and scrape out the seeds into the milk. Bring the mixture to the boil, then turn down the heat to minimum.

2 Whisk the egg yolks and caster sugar together in a bowl until they are pale in colour and very light. Pour the hot cream into the eggs, whisking as you do so. (The cream must NOT be boiling.) Then you can either return the mixture to the saucepan and cook over a very low heat, stirring it constantly and watching it carefully to ensure that it never boils, or if you feel more cautious, use a double saucepan (bain-marie). The custard is cooked when it is smooth, lump-free and forms a ribbon as it falls from the spoon.

3 Finally, whisk in the mustard, brown sugar and honey. Allow to cool. When cold, churn in an ice cream machine until frozen according to the maker's instructions.

θεβανι ηπειρωτικο
spiced syrup cake

This is a seriously ymmy cake from Epirus. It is very rich and sticky.

220g butter, plus a little to grease
   the tin
220g caster sugar
5 medium eggs, separated
240g plain flour
240g coarse semolina
2 teaspoons baking powder
1 teaspoon bicarbonate of soda
150g almonds, finely chopped
2 vanilla pods

SOAKING SYRUP
700g sugar
1–3 litres water
1 orange, juice and zest
1 x 3cm cinnamon stick
8 cloves
2 lemons, juice and zest

1 To prepare the syrup, combine the sugar with the water in a saucepan. Cook over low heat until the sugar has dissolved, then add the cinnamon stick, cloves, fruit juice and zest.

2 Leave to simmer for 20 minutes. Remove the flavourings and allow to cool.

3 Preheat your oven to 180°C/350°F/Gas 4.

4 Use an electric mixer to beat the butter in a bowl until it is light and fluffy. Gradually add the sugar, beating at a medium speed.

5 Add the egg yolks to the bowl, one at a time, beating very well after each addition. Meanwhile, sift the flour, semolina, bicarbonate of soda and baking powder together in a bowl. Very gradually add them to the cake batter, continuing to beat at medium speed.

6 Add the finely chopped almonds to the bowl and scrape the seeds from the vanilla pods into the mixture. Give the batter one last turn on very high speed for a few seconds. Put to one side.

7 Beat the egg whites in a bowl to meringue point (soft, white peaks) and fold the mixture into the cake batter slowly, and a little at a time, as you would do for a soufflé.

8 Pour the batter into a buttered 25cm cake tin and bake in the centre of the oven for about 50 minutes, or until the cake springs back when touched lightly with your fingertips.

9 Remove the cake from the oven and place the tin on a cake rack. Use a sharp, paring knife to score the cake deeply in diamond shapes across the top. Pour the cool syrup over the entire cake and allow to cool down as the syrup soaks in.

συκαλακια γεμιστα στον φουρνο
baked stuffed figs

The dried fruit give away the provenance of this dish which comes from the Mironty in Western Turkey.

MAKES ENOUGH FOR ABOUT
4 X 500G JARS (DEPENDING ON
THE SIZE OF YOUR FIGS)

2kg large, fresh figs

300g walnuts, coarsely chopped

200g almonds, coarsely chopped

2 x 4cm cinnamon sticks, finely
   ground

1 teaspoon clove powder

4 tablespoons sesame seeds

4 bay leaves

6 fresh basil stalks

1 Place the figs in a large saucepan and cover them with cold water. Put a plate on the top of them to keep them submerged and allow them to soak for 5 hours.

2 Preheat your oven to 150°C/300°F/Gas 2.

3 Check that the figs haven't soaked up all the water and if necessary, add a little more so that they are still covered. Bring to the boil, then put the lid on and cook for 3 minutes.

4 Remove the saucepan from the heat and leave it, still covered, to cool.

5 Meanwhile, take a bowl and mix together the nuts, cinnamon, clove powder and the sesame seeds.

6 Remove the figs from the water. Open out the small hole at the top where the stem joins and stuff the figs with the nut mixture. Close the top of each fig with your fingertips.

7 Place the figs on a small, greased roasting tray and bake them for 1 hour, or until they feel dry. When cold, transfer to sterilized preserving jars with the bay leaves and basil stems. They will keep for a couple of months. Store in the fridge once open. Eat them with yoghurt and honey.

etceteras

THIS SECTION CONTAINS A MIXTURE OF STORECUPBOARD STAPLES,

PRESERVES, SIDE DISHES AND ACCOMPANIMENTS. SERVING SIZES ARE NOT

ALWAYS GIVEN SINCE OFTEN A LARGE BATCH FOR STORING IS PREPARED.

artichoke and garden pea casserole

αρακας με αγγιναρες

This dish belongs to a group which are known as "ladera", or more literally, dishes made with oil. In fact, this is something of a misnomer because although they are very rich, they do not end up oily.

1kg fresh peas in the pod
6 globe artichokes
3 whole lemons
175ml olive oil
1 bunch spring onions, trimmed and chopped (including the green parts)
Juice of 2 lemons
2 heaped tablespoons finely chopped fresh dill
Sea salt and freshly ground black pepper

1 Pod the peas, wash and strain them.

2 To prepare the artichokes, first cut off the stem of each one to leave about 3cm and then peel the remaining stem. Take off the outer two rings of leaves and slice the artichoke across to separate the base from the leaves. Trim it back to reveal the hairy "choke" in the centre of the bud. Remove it carefully with a teaspoon. Each artichoke must be rubbed over with half a lemon and then kept in water to which a squeeze of lemon has been added. (The acidulated water stops them oxidizing and going black.)

3 Take a large pot and add 100ml of the oil. Sweat the spring onions in the oil gently until they begin to soften. Add the peas and season to taste.

4 Strain the artichokes and rinse well in fresh water. Put the artichokes "face down" (i.e. stems upward!) on top of the peas. Add the lemon juice and 250ml hot water and the rest of the olive oil. Cover the pan and leave to simmer for 20 minutes.

5 Add a further 250ml hot water and the chopped dill. Cook gently until the artichokes are done (they should be soft like potatoes which are ready for mashing), and all the water is absorbed and the vegetables left in the oil.

simple pilaff

ασπρο πιλαφι

This rice pilaff is good with any dish that has plenty of gravy.

SERVES 4

600ml chicken stock (or water)
250g long grain rice
25g butter
1 teaspoon salt

1 Pour the stock into a saucepan and bring to the boil. Skim it and add the rice and salt. Stir thoroughly and then cook, covered, on the top of the stove for 15 minutes, or until the rice has absorbed all the liquid. Do not stir.

2 Remove from the heat, stir in the butter and cover with a clean, wet tea towel. Leave for 10 minutes before serving.

lahano pilaff

λαχανοπιλαφο

The Lahano cabbage is a large, pale green cabbage which looks rather like a Savoy cabbage that has had all its wrinkles ironed out, and has then been sat on until flattened out. You will find Lahano at good Greek, Middle-Eastern and Cypriot greengrocers. If you haven't got access to such a shop, use one of the substitutes below. This pilaff is the traditional accompaniment to the dish of stewed crab claws on page 86.

1.2kg Lahano cabbage (or another pale, soft cabbage such as January King or Savoy)
100g butter
500g Greek short-grain rice or risotto rice
100ml dry white wine
Juice of 2 lemons
2 tablespoons cold butter
Sea salt and freshly ground black pepper

1 Put the whole cabbage into a large pot, fill with water and add 1 dessertspoon salt. Leave to simmer for 30–45 minutes, by which time the cabbage should be very soft and the water will taste cabbagy.

2 Lift out the cabbage, draining the water back into the pot. Place the cabbage on a chopping board and turn the heat under the pot right up so that the water boils while you cut out the core and shred the cabbage.

3 In a large, hot frying pan melt the butter until it browns and sizzles, then add the shredded cabbage and the rice. Keep stirring for 3 or 4 minutes until the rice gets well coated in the nutty brown butter.

4 Pour in the white wine, which will be absorbed immediately.

5 Start to add the cabbage water in much the same way as you would when making risotto: a little at a time, as each ladle of water is soaked up. You are aiming for cooked rice and a "sloppy" textured pilaff so just before you reach that point, add the lemon juice and season to taste with salt (if necessary), also freshly ground black pepper.

6 Finally, stir in the cold butter and serve.

"By its fruit a tree is known"

(when bargaining with the fruit sellers)

pickled celery

A light and delicious pickle.

1 head of celery (including the
   leafy bits)
100ml extra virgin olive oil
Juice of 2 lemons
a bulb of fennel (including the
   leafy bits), chopped
1 teaspoon fresh thyme leaves
1 heaped tablespoon chopped
   flat-leaf parsley
2 bay leaves
Sea salt and freshly ground black
   pepper

1 Peel the backs of the celery stalks to remove their strings and cut them into
4cm lengths.

2 Take a pot large enough to hold all the celery and combine the oil, lemon
juice, fennel, thyme, parsley and bay leaves and about 100ml of boiling water
in it. Season well with salt and pepper and bring to the boil.

3 Drop in the celery and add more boiling water until the celery is just about
submerged. Put a plate on top of the celery to keep it submerged, turn down
the heat and simmer for 10–15 minutes, or until the celery is just softening
but still firm.

4 Remove the pot from the heat and allow the celery to cool in the liquid.

5 Pack the celery into preserving jars treated with sterilizing solution or
run them through the dishwasher (remember to remove the rubber seals).
Cover with the liquid. You can boil the liquid down to reduce if there is much
too much of it.

6 Open after three weeks. Keep in the fridge for up to 14 days once open.
Eat with cold meats.

σαλτσα ντοματας
tomato sauce

This sauce will keep for months provided that every time you spoon some out, you make good the olive oil seal across the top by smoothing out the solid oil with the back of a spoon. If the urge to pickle and preserve strikes you in September when tomatoes are plentiful and full-flavoured, buy a box and make this in bulk.

2kg ripe plum tomatoes (if you are in the wrong season, use 1kg of good passata)

4 cloves of garlic, peeled but left whole

3 bay leaves

3cm of cinnamon stick

250g shallots, peeled and sliced lengthways, but not chopped

230ml olive oil

Sea salt and freshly ground black pepper

1 Skin the tomatoes by scoring them and dropping them into boiling water and counting to ten. Drain and rub the skin off. De-seed and roughly chop them up.

2 Put them into a large pot with the garlic, bay leaves and cinnamon.

3 Add enough water to barely cover them and bring to the boil. Skim, then turn the heat down and cook for 20 minutes, skimming occasionally.

4 Add the shallots and cook on, uncovered, until they are soft, about 35–45 minutes. By then the tomatoes should have lost most of their water and the sauce will have started to thicken. Season and stir in 200ml olive oil. Cook for 15–20 minutes.

5 Remove the sauce from the heat and while it is still hot, put it into a sterilized preserving jar. Float the remaining olive oil across the surface of the sauce to act as a seal. Allow to cool and store in the fridge where it will keep for 3–4 months.

ζεστος πουρες μελιτζανας
warm purée of aubergines

This dish adopts the role of vegetable side dish with all kinds of meats and poultry.

700g aubergines

25ml whole milk

25ml double cream

75g butter

1 nutmeg, grated

1 heaped tablespoon finely chopped flat-leaf parsley,

Sea salt and freshly ground black pepper

1 Char the aubergines thoroughly (either over a gas burner, on a barbecue or under the grill). When blackened, put them into a plastic bag and leave to cool. When cool, they will peel easily.

2 Chop the aubergine pulp and then use either a pestle and mortar or a food processor/blender to reduce to a purée. Heat the milk, cream, butter and nutmeg in a saucepan and add the aubergine pulp. Simmer together for 15 minutes while it thickens slightly.

3 Transfer to a serving dish. Taste and season with salt and pepper.

4 Serve dressed with a small mound of chopped parsley.

trahanas τραχανας

There is no substitute for trahanas, which is a kind of pasta made from ewes' milk. It is formed into tiny needles about the same size and shape as grains of rice, and is cooked in a way that is a cross between risotto and couscous.

SERVES 4

100g butter
90ml extra virgin olive oil
250g trahanas
500ml hot chicken stock
500ml goats' milk, heated
250g feta cheese, crumbled
a little hot milk, if needed
100ml olive oil
100g cherry tomatoes
100g Kalamata olives
250g rocket
Sea salt and freshly ground black
pepper

1 Melt half the butter in a heavy saucepan and add the extra virgin olive oil. Pre-cook the trahanas gently as if you were making risotto until it is a light golden brown.

2 Pour in the stock and goats' milk and leave to simmer with the lid on for 15 minutes. Stir occasionally.

3 Add the crumbled feta and simmer for another 10 minutes or until the trahana is tender and the majority of the liquid has been absorbed. The texture should be that of a well-made risotto - no drier. Taste, and it will probably not need much more seasoning because of the cheese – but if it does, add salt and pepper at this point. In case the trahanas becomes too thick have a little hot milk on standby.

4 Stir in the remaining butter before serving. Heat the olive oil in a frying pan, add the cherry tomatoes and olives, and then cook for 10 minutes over a medium heat. Add the rocket and quickly wilt it. Place the rocket and tomato mixture on top of the trahana and serve.

mustard mayonnaise μαγιονεζα με μουσταρδα

A tangy mayonnaise with a pleasant bite.

25g dry English mustard (more if
you wish for even more punch)
1 tablespoon fresh lemon juice
3 medium eggs (2 separated,
1 whole)
250ml light vegetable oil
250ml olive oil
2 tablespoons white wine vinegar
Sea salt and freshly ground black
pepper

Method for a mixing bowl and whisk

1 Start by mixing together the mustard and lemon juice in a bowl.
2 Add 2 egg yolks and mix well.
3 Mix the two lots of oil together in a jug and start to add them a drop at a time to the egg mixture, whisking as you go.
4 Finally, add the white wine vinegar and then the remaining whole egg. Season to taste.

Method for a food processor

1 Start by mixing together the mustard and the lemon juice.
2 Add the 2 egg yolks and process again to mix together well.
3 Mix the two lots of oil together in a jug and start to add this in a gentle stream as the machine is running.
4 Finally, add the white wine vinegar and then the remaining whole egg. Season to taste.

λικερ με ζαφορα
homemade saffron liqueur

This works best when made with a fierce and fiery spirit like Raki (a kind of Greek Grappa). However, if you cannot obtain it, using Ouzo will add a further layer of flavour to the finished drink.

1 bottle Raki (if unavailable, use
  Ouzo)
1 teaspoon cracked coriander
  seeds
1 teaspoon cloves
2 cinnamon sticks
1 nutmeg, cracked into pieces
  with a hammer!
0.5g saffron
100g sugar

1 Put the bottle of Raki into a 1 litre preserving jar with the coriander, cloves, cinnamon sticks, nutmeg and saffron. Seal and keep in a cool place for 40 days, shaking the bottle occasionally.
2 Sieve out the aromatics from the bottle and add the sugar gradually, tasting as you go. You may find that 100g is too much.
3 Serve in a small glass with an ice cube.

home-salted cod

σπιτικος μπακαλιαρος αλμυρος

If you cannot eat the whole piece of cod at a sitting, it will keep for at least a week. Simply brush the fish all over with olive oil, wrap in cling film and refrigerate.

400g sugar
600g sea salt
3 heaped tablespoons flat-leaf
    parsley, chopped
1kg thick fillet of cod, pin-boned
    (ask your fishmonger)

1 Mix the sugar, salt and parsley together in a bowl thoroughly.
2 Take a suitably sized plastic container (use one which has a lid) and spread one third of the mixture evenly over the bottom. Put the cod fillet on top of the mixture and cover with the remainder. Replace the lid and keep in the fridge for at least 24 hours, turning the fillet over once. (You can leave the cod in the cure for up to 3 days.)
3 Rinse the cod thoroughly before use.

fricassee of green dandelion leaves

φρικασε με αγρια ραδικια

Now you can see for yourself why rabbits so enjoy dandelions.

SERVES 6

1kg of green dandelion leaves,
    roots trimmed and washed
    very well (if not available, look
    for curly endive leaves)
1kg leeks trimmed, rinsed well
    and cut into 3 or 4 smaller
    pieces
1kg Cos lettuce, washed very well,
    and cut into 3 equal pieces
130ml olive oil
Juice of 1 small lemon
50g dill, finely chopped
Sea salt and freshly ground black
    pepper

1 Drop the dandelion leaves or curly endive into a saucepan of boiling water and blanch with the lid on for 5 minutes.
2 Drain the blanching water and put the dandelion leaves or endive back in the same pot. Add the leeks and 1 litre of boiling water. Place the lid back on the pot and cook over medium heat for 20 minutes.
3 Add the Cos lettuce, mix everything well and put the lid back on. Keep cooking over the same heat for 40 minutes, by which time the leeks should look very tender and be falling apart and the vegetable broth should taste slightly sweet with a pleasant bitter aftertaste, which will be coming from the dandelion leaves.
4 Add seasoning and the olive oil, and cook for 15 more minutes. Remove from the heat and add the lemon juice and the chopped dill. Give it a good stir and serve.

endive fricassee

"Bitter endive meets delicate Cos" – a good marriage.

SERVES 4

1 head of curly-leaved endive
   (frisée)
1 head of Cos lettuce
1kg leeks (the white parts only)
100ml extra virgin olive oil
1 heaped tablespoon finely
   chopped flat-leaf parsley
Juice of 1 lemon
Sea salt and freshly ground black
   pepper

1 Remove the coarse outer leaves from the endive and discard. Separate the inner leaves and blanch them in boiling water for about 5 minutes; reserve.
2 Slice the lettuce across into 3cm pieces. Wash and drain it thoroughly.
3 Chop the leeks into 2cm disks and wash and drain thoroughly.
4 Put half the olive oil into a heavy-bottomed pot. Add the leeks, lettuce and endive, and 150ml water; season. Put the lid back on and braise gently until meltingly soft, about 45–60 minutes.
5 Add the chopped flat-leaf parsley, the remaining oil and the lemon juice. Leave to simmer for a further 15 minutes. Serve warm with a lemon wedge.

anchovy pâté

This dish is best made with the strongly flavoured salted anchovy fillets (be sure to rinse them well), but the anchovies from tins or jars will do as well. You can either use a food processor or pound everything with a pestle and mortar. This paste will keep for several weeks in the fridge and is served on bread or biscuits.

200g anchovies
50g capers
150g mixed pickled vegetables
2 heaped tablespoons finely
   chopped, fresh flat-leaf parsley
200ml extra virgin olive oil
1 tablespoon white wine vinegar

Method for a pestle and mortar

1 Work the anchovies, capers, vegetables and herbs together to a paste.
2 Add the oil and finally, the vinegar. You should end up with a thick, pungent paste.

Method for a food processor

1 Start by adding the anchovies to the bowl. Process and then stream in the oil.
2 Add the other ingredients and process again to finish up with the same result as above.

meat stock for poaching

A good, wholesome stock – supermarket stock makes an acceptable substitute, but nothing beats homemade.

1 large Spanish onion
2 bay leaves
1kg beef shin or veal bones

1 Skin the onion and cut it in half. Grill it until the flesh has coloured, but not burnt (this will not take long).
2 Put the onion with the bay leaves and the shin or bones into a large stockpot and cover with water.
3 Bring to the boil, turn down the heat and leave to simmer for 3 hours.
4 Cool, cover and then refrigerate. The next day remove the fat from the surface of the stock.

pickled green peppers

You can buy these in jars if you cannot face making your own.

1kg long, green peppers (you'll find them in Greek, Middle Eastern or Turkish delicatessens, as well as some supermarkets)
1 litre good quality white wine vinegar
75g coarse sea salt

1 Pierce each pepper with the tip of a sharp knife in two or three places. Place them in a jar with plenty of water and leave them for 4–5 days. Change the water regularly.
2 Strain off the water and put the peppers back in the jar. Add the vinegar and the salt. Place something heavy on the top to keep the peppers submerged. Leave them in the pickling liquid for at least a week before eating them.
3 Store them in the fridge. Once open, they will keep for several weeks.

the greek
storecupboard

storecupboard

Avgotaraho This is delicious. It is the dried and salted roe of a particular kind of mullet which enters the brackish waters of Lake Messolonghi to spawn. The nearest thing to it is the highly-prized Italian dried grey mullet roe called bottarga, but connoisseurs rate the Greek roe more highly, perhaps because the Italian mullet are strictly saltwater fish.

Cod's roe If you can get plain, salted cod's roe from your fishmonger do so, but it is quite all right to substitute the smoked cod's roe that is widely available.

Fava These are simple, yellow split peas. The best are said to come from Santorini, where the volcanic soil makes for very good, strongly flavoured pulses. Standard yellow dal from Asian shops or supermarkets makes an acceptable substitute.

Feta cheese There have been a succession of court cases over the right of cheesemakers to make "feta" outside Greece. And there is a lot of mass-market feta style cheese made, particularly in Scandinavia. Before leaping to any conclusions, however, you owe it to yourself to try the real thing. Genuine Greek feta is matured in wooden barrels and has an astonishing depth of flavour. Look for it in specialist cheese shops, the smarter supermarkets and Greek shops. Ordinary feta is a pale imitation, but the only substitute there is.

Filo You can make filo for yourself if you have flour, a pasta machine, the time and patience, and the recipe on page 132 (there are some recipes where the thicker homemade filo outperforms the shop-bought kind).

However, for most practical purposes the ready-made filo which is available from supermarkets and delicatessens will be fine. You can identify the better brands by looking out for a short shelf life. Fresh is good! The only thing you must bear in mind is that any filo dries out quickly, becoming brittle and unmanageable. Leave a sheet of filo out for two minutes and it becomes useless, so keep any unused filo under a damp cloth while you deal with each sheet.

Gigandes In Greek shops you may find the beans called Gigandes, which is why the classic dish on page 57 is called Gigandes Plaki. The best beans come from Macedonia and Epirus. When the new season's supply arrives in the shops in the autumn, they are sweeter and less tough than those which have sat around since the year before. If you cannot find Gigandes, butter beans or cannellini beans come a poor second.

Glyko This is a very sweet preserve, sometimes known as "spoon sweets" because you eat them straight off a spoon with your afternoon coffee.

Graviera cheese A firm cheese that is close in texture to Gruyère and moderately salty. Good for cooking with, but Gruyère would make an acceptable substitute.

Honey Greek honey is some of the finest in the world. This is because there are no huge fields of commercial crops like rapeseed, whose blossom attracts the bees but whose nectar taints the honey. Greek thyme honey is particularly fine and when the thyme stops flowering at the end of the season the bees go on to make pine tree honey which is also good and especially rich in minerals. Insist on Greek honey and look out for the brand name Odysea.

Kaseri cheese A mild, cheese that is smooth and creamy in character.

Kefalotiri cheese You may find this cheese in specialist delicatessens. It is a cheese with a brilliant texture, but is not widely available. Substitute the Italian cheese, Pecorino, which has many similar characteristics.

Krithiraki This is actually a pasta, although each tiny shard is about the same size and shape as a grain of rice. It is usually served "sloppy" and makes a grand accompaniment to stews.

Lahano This is large, flat-headed white cabbage which is found all over the Mediterranean. You can sometimes find it in Greek or Turkish grocery shops. Deciding on a good substitute depends on which function the cabbage is fulfilling. Shredded in a pilaff and you could get away with Savoy cabbage, but when you want a flat leaf to wrap around a filling, the large, outer leaves of Cos lettuce would be a better bet.

Lakerda This is a fish known in Greece as the "gold grey" mullet. To prepare Lakerda, the whole fish are packed upside down in a barrel full of salt. A weight is added to press the fish and they are left to cure for ten days. At the end of this period the fish are washed and then dried for three days. Finally, they are smoked over a wood chip fire. There is no obvious substitute, although smoked mackerel would be similar.

Lentils Use small, greeny-brown lentils. There has recently been a vogue for "designer" lentils from Umbria in Italy or Puy in France. The best Greek lentils come from Macedonia.

Lumpfish roe Caviar will always be caviar, but such is mankind's cavalier attitude to nature that it is fast disappearing (something which contributes to its soaring price). Fortunately, most of the Greek recipes from the minority that demand caviar work as well with the more prosaically named lumpfish roe. The black lumpfish roe that is sold in small jars is merely orange roe dyed black, but by mixing the two you can get a pretty effect.

Manouri cheese A soft and sweet cheese; a kind of Greek "cream cheese with attitude". Ordinary cream cheese would make an acceptable subsitute.

Octopus It's confusing, but there are two different octopi – on the one hand is the Eastern Atlantic octopus and on the other is the "red" or Mediterranean octopus, which can be distinguished by the double row of suckers it has on each tentacle. Octopus can be bought from good fishmongers and supermarkets, and often comes frozen in 1kg blocks, which are fine when properly thawed.

Olives The Greeks have spent the last 1,000 years tending olive groves and, with some justification, they feel that they are getting quite good at it! Greek olives are the product of a winning combination: traditional skills and modern machinery and know-how. Look for the brand names Karyatis and Rovies when buying olives, and do not ignore the supermarket "own label" Greek olives, which are of extremely high quality.

Olive oil Greek extra virgin olive oil has a rich, grassy character all of its own and represents remarkably good value when you compare it with the fashionable Italian and Spanish oils. Brands to look out for are Karyatis and Iliada, although the supermarket's own label Greek oils usually offer very high quality at bargain prices. As a general principle, it makes sense to have two differing olive oils in the kitchen cupboard – a basic one for cooking with, and a more characterful (and expensive) extra virgin oil for dressings, and drizzling over a finished dish on occasions when there is no fierce heat to destroy the bouquet.

Pastourma This cured meat was originally made with fillet of camel, which was rubbed with pungent spices and buried in a hole in the ground! Now it is made from fillet of beef and is a kind of bresaola with attitude.

Pickled red peppers These are very tasty! They come in jars and are sweet and smoky to the tongue. You'll find them in Greek shops and in an increasing number of supermarkets.

Pistachios The cuisine of the Greek minority in Turkey uses a lot of pistachios, and rather naturally they insist on Greek nuts! Greek pistachios are longer and glossier, and the best ones come from the island of Aegina.

Raki This is Greek firewater. It is a bold spirit that goes well with smoked fish and has a distinctive, almost aniseedy tang to it. Very strong indeed.

Rice This is one of the staples of Greek cuisine and there are three or four varieties. For the chicken soup (page 55) you need the kind known as "round" rice. In practice, this is much the same as Italian risotto rice, which makes a fine substitute. The third best option is regular short-grain rice, and long-grain rice should be avoided for these dishes.

Saffron Greek saffron is always of the highest quality. When you are paying so much for such a small quantity of spice, any economies are usually false ones.

Remember that all spices lose flavour with age and this season's saffron is better than last season's. For once it is worth picking the pack with the longest "best before" date. Saffron usually comes in small plastic boxes containing 1g, which makes measuring easier.

Vinegar If you have a Greek delicatessen you may well be able to get Greek aged wine vinegar. This is an organic product with an amazing depth of flavour, and unlike some of the cheaper balsamic vinegars that are taking over the shelves, no caramel is used in its production. If you cannot find this admittedly rare product, substitute a good quality red wine vinegar rather than the more syrupy balsamic.

Vine leaves Picked vine leaves (vital for making dolmades as few of us can stroll onto the terrace and pick leaves from our own vines) come in flat packs, brined in jars, or salted and dried (which are the best). Remember to rinse them well to get rid of as much of the salt as possible.

Walnuts Nuts are seasonal delicacies. Always try and be sure that the walnuts you buy are as fresh as possible.

Yoghurt Everyone comes back from their first holiday in Greece singing the praises of Greek yoghurt eaten with a little honey as a breakfast dish. Now this rich style of yoghurt is available in the U.K. Look out for the brand names Total (also known as Fage) and Delta. Greek yoghurt is a natural product and mass market cow's milk yoghurt makes a poor substitute.

mail order

Greek produce is making significant inroads into the major supermarkets so unless you have your own favourite Greek shop or enlightened delicatessen, it is always worth enquiring about particular Greek foods. In the event that locating ingredients is difficult, there is always mail order. For a wide range of genuine Greek produce by mail order, contact Panos Manuelides at Odysea, 2/3 Charterhouse Square, London EC3 6EE (020 7251 0404). Gigandes beans, rice, olives, olive oil, thyme honey, saffron, roasted red peppers, preserved vine leaves .... Or contact the Real Greek website at www.therealgreek.co.uk

wine

The resurgence of Greek wines in the UK has been a wonderful sight to behold. Where once there was just Retsina, there is now an imposing array of winemakers creating wines that are the envy of many older, established wine producing countries. It seems as if the range of Greek wines increases month on month and year on year, so by way of guidelines here are some names to look out for. They all make wines that have distinguished themselves with the customers at the Real Greek restaurant, wines which are unlikely to disappoint, however sophisticated your palate.

Antonopoulos From the Peloponnese. Look out for high quality Cabernet "New Oak" and the Chardonnay, both of which are made in the "French" style. Also worth noting are whites like the Roditis Alepou and Adoli-Ghis, and the red Ampelochora.

Averoff A producer based in Epirus to the north-west of Athens. They blend traditional Greek grape varieties with proven European ones. Note the rich, red Katogi and the subtle white Traminer.

Boutari A famous name in Greek wine making, and one which is linked with two separate wine making operations (see Kyr-Yiannis). The Naoussa Grand Reserve is a full red wine from Naoussa; the Moscofilero is a floral, white wine from Mantinea.

Gaia Estate From the Peloponnese, the Gaia Estate has been shot into the limelight with an amazing tally of medals at International wine fairs. Look out for the pale Notios white and the rich Notios red (notios means "from the South"); also Thalassitis red and white.

Hazimichalis From Atlantis. A wide range of wines including some that are very traditionally made. Choose the Athiri-Asyrtiko or the aromatic Sauvignon Blanc Fumé.

Kyr-Yiannis Yiannis Boutari is known for his ultra modern winery and his Ramnista, a heavy red wine.

Lazaridis From Drama in Macedonia. Produces an excellent rosé and also Château Julia Chardonnay. Greenish in colour and buttery to taste.

Mercouri Estate Wines from the west coast of the Peloponnese. Known for the highly acclaimed Domaine Mercouri, an outstanding red wine made from a mix of Refosco and Mavrodaphne grapes.

Skouras From Argos in the Peloponnese. Another producer who has adopted French techniques. They make a fine Viognier, a Cambello, and a red and white Megas Oenos – the red is very fine indeed.

Spiropolous From the Peloponnese. The Spiropolous Mantinea is an elegant, organically made white wine. Pale and flinty.

greek wine specialists

It would be impossible to list every specialist stockist of Greek wines in the United Kingdom, but as well as a growing representation in the wine departments of the major supermarkets, here are two sources you can rely on:

Enotika Wine Cellars, 19 St Leonard's Road, Far Cotton, Northampton NN4 8DL (01604 675522).

Oddbins – over 240 stores nationwide – ring 020 8944 4400 for details.

www.therealgreek.co.uk

"Wine speaks its own language, it's a pity more people don't understand what it says"

acknowledgement:

To my parents, whose love of good food still inspires me.

Our thanks to
Susan Campbell, Janie Suthering and Sandra
Purkess for grappling with the recipes.

Gus Filgate and Peter Thompson for
stunning photographs, and Paul Welti for
making the book look so good.

Zoe Antoniou and all at Pavilion for their
patience.

Panos Manuelides for supplies.

Paloma Campbell for her knowledge of
Greek wines.

And a special thank you to the backbone of
the Real Greek kitchen brigade, Amanda
Murphy, Alasdair Fraser, and Jodi Parsons.

Theodore & Charles

IN SEPTEMBER 1999 THE REAL GREEK RESTAURANT OPENED AT 15 HOXTON MARKET,

LONDON N1 6HG (020 7739 8212) TO A WAVE OF SPECTACULARLY GOOD REVIEWS. AT

THE 60-SEATER RESTAURANT THEODORE KYRIAKOU AND HIS BUSINESS PARTNER PALOM

CAMPBELL CONTINUE TO OFFER BOTH REAL GREEK FOOD AND A REAL GREEK WELCOME

index